P9-CFR-131

CLASSIC QUILTS
Contemporary Style

Classic Quilts Contemporary Style
Japanese Title: Washizawa Reiko No Hoshini Negaio
Copyright © 2007 Reiko Washizawa
Originally published in Japanese language by Japan Broadcast Publishing Co.,
Ltd. (NHK Publishing Co., Ltd.)
English language licensed by World Book Media, LLC
For international rights inquiries contact: info@worldbookmedia.com

All rights reserved. The written instructions, photographs, designs, patterns,
and projects in this volume are intended for the personal use of the reader and
may be reproduced for that purpose only. Any other use, especially commercial
use, is forbidden under law without the express written permission of the
copyright holder. Violators will be prosecuted to the fullest extent of the law. No
other part of this book may be reproduced in any form or by any electronic or
mechanical means including information storage and retrieval systems without
permission in writing from the publisher, excerpt by a reviewer, who may quote
a brief passage in review.

www.fwmedia.com

First published in the United States of America by Krause Publications,
an imprint of F+W Media, Inc., 4700 East Galbraith Rd., Cincinnati, Ohio 45236
(800) 289-0963. First edition 2010.

Printed in China

Library of Congress Cataloging-in-Publication Data
Washizawa, Reiko.
Classic quilts contemporary style / Reiko Washizawa.
p. cm.
Includes index.
ISBN-13: 978-1-4402-0822-5 (pbk. : alk. paper)
ISBN-10: 1-4402-0822-0 (pbk. : alk. paper)
1. Patchwork—Patterns. 2. Quilting—Patterns. 3. Stars in art. I.Title.
TT835.W3733 2010
746.46'041—dc22
2009050534

10 9 8 7 6 5 4 3 2 1

CLASSIC QUILTS
Contemporary Style

 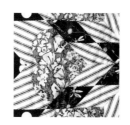 

Reiko Washizawa

Cincinnati, Ohio

Contents

Author's Note

The works in this book can be loosely sorted into three categories. The first is slightly larger quilts used in everyday life, such as bedcovers, blankets, and throws. The second is miniature tapestries, which can hang on a wall as decoration. (These miniature quilts can also be sewn into handbags.) The third is round-robin quilts, created by a group of quilters. These are similar to friendship quilts, which are made by having all of your friends bring together their own patterns and assembling them into one piece, or a signature quilt, on which friends sew their signatures for a celebration or anniversary.

Because a round-robin quilt is passed around, the number of people who will be contributing and the size of the completed piece is decided in advance. The first person sews the center piece, establishing the design and color palette. When the center piece is complete, it is passed on to the second person who adds to the design in their own way. It is then passed on to the next person and the next, each quilter using their own creative contribution, finally resulting in a complete quilt. There are many quilts which can be made by oneself, but quilts that are created collaboratively can be just as enjoyable.

For this book, I have tapped the talents of many of my students and enjoyed helping them complete these beautiful quilts. I am happy to be introducing all of you, as well, to the joys of quilting.

Reiko Washizawa

Part I

Gallery of Quilts

Five-Point Compass I

This Five-Point Compass pattern features layered stars at the center. To soften the hard edges of the geometric design, delicate floral appliqués have been added.

Instructions: page 61

Artists: Naoko Iwamura Reiko Ebata Yōko Kaku Jyunko Kirihara Mitsue Sakuma Yuami Takeuchi Kazuko Harada Keiko Fujinawa Ritsuko Machida Sonoko Matsumoto Atsuko Yoshida

Instructions: page 61

Similar to the Five-Point Compass I, this design uses green fabric accents and green thread for softness. Surrounding this Five-Point Compass is a frame of glittering Friendship Stars.

Artists: Tomoko Akatsu Kazuko Itabashi Sadako Okada Kayo Okamoto Fumiyo Sawamoto Hiroko Shinpo Yōko Takeo Chihaya Hashimoto

Feathered Star

Outlining the center star is a toothy ("feathered") edge, which is balanced by a cute flower motif. Hexagonal stars anchor the corners of the design.

Instructions: page 172

Artists: Asako Ishizuka Sumiyo Irie Haruyo Ueda Noriko Satō Miyoko Harada Toshie Yokoyama Kiyoko Wakabayashi

Instructions: page 174

In this traditional American design, four large eight-point stars surround a four-point star. Positive and negative space create the illusion of even more stars. More four-point stars anchor the corners of the border, in which diagonal color tiles create movement.

Artists: Sakiko Shitamura Naoko Suzuki Kyōko Tanikami Yōko Nakano Hatsuko Narita Naoko Hoshino

Rising Star

This design celebrates the first star to rise in the evening sky. Inlaid with dozens of other starbursts of color, this star-studded quilt evokes the night sky.

Instructions: page 182

Artists: Tomoko Akiba Yasuko Ōno Yōko Kawazu Sayoko Koshinuma Kimiko Sakakibara Fumiko Shimizu Shinobu Minagawa

Instructions: page 170

Choose shades of red and orange fabric for a powerful sun, and celebrate the harvest with winding flowers and leaves.

Artists: Hitomi Arai Ritsuko Ojima Machiko Suzuki Yōko Kondo Kayoko Nasu Keiko Hayashi Michiko Maebashi Yōko Mabuchi Chiyoko Watanabe

Larger Quilts

Castle Wall

In this pattern, glittering stars shine at the corners of the quilt's window panes.
Because this is a bold pattern, a simple color scheme will have the strongest effect.

Instructions: page 146

Artist: Keiko Nakamura

Round-Robin Quilts

Eternal Blossom

This star-square hybrid that seems to radiate light is called the romantic Eternal Blossom. Framed by rosebuds, the finished design evokes a flower garden.

Instructions: page 184

Artists: Toshiko Ikeda Yōko Izumi Yasuko Ooya Shitsuko Satō Mieko Nishioka Hiromi Nishiwaki Naoko Masuda Emiko Matoba

Instructions: page 180

This quilt is assembled from a variety of scrap cloth, with the star fashioned from several triangles. Bolder colors are used in the center of the star so that the shape of the pinwheel stands out clearly.

Artists: Yasuyo Kikuchi Yōko Koizumi Chieko Kotegawa Emiko Hanano Setsuko Fukuda Mitsuko Furukawa Atsuko Watai

Broken Star

This expansive design features waves of increasing brightness, which mimic radiating light. With flower appliqués nestled between the rings of color, the celestial becomes floral.

Artists: Yasuko Uchibori Noriko Endo Hiroko Okada Michiyo Kobori Shigeko Satō Misako Tomioka Yuriko Miyazaki Fumiko Kometani

Instructions: page 176

Instructions: page 168

This distinctly American design features a central diamond rimmed on all four sides by triangles, which align into a basic star shape. A soft color scheme with bold details highlights the squares-and-stripes geometric frames.

Artists: Yasuko Ochi Mitsuko Seki Terumi Takagi Yōko Nakayama Kumi Hashimoto Kimiko Maruyama Mitsuko Yoshino

Larger Quilts

Lone Star

The soft, simple color palette lets the dozens of identical stars speak for themselves.

Instructions: page 156

Artist: Isako Murakami

Flying Swallows

Within a large star, eight swallows fly in formation.
At the corners, swallow appliqués watch as the
quilt's flock flies south for the winter.

Instructions: page 178

Artists: Kaori Kata Shizue Suzuki Hiroko Suzuki Ichiko Nagase Chiemi Mikami Kazumi Yasuoka Mariko Watanabe

Instructions: page 166

Five stars cluster in the center of this design. The generous border is formed from a stylized, appliquéd tulip design.

Artists: Akiko Sakurai Mitsuko Takita Hiromi Tachi Hisako Fukuoka Noriko Fukumoto Mariko Fuchigami Mayumi Mifune Kuniyo Yamada

Star of Bethlehem

In the center of the Star of Bethlehem, a flower basket appliqué rests on a field of simple, white fabric. The candy-striped borders and winding holly vine create a classic holiday quilt design.

Instructions: page 164

Artists: Akemi Akiyama Kazuko Ishii Keiko Nozaki Mayumi Honma Yuuko Yamaguchi Rika Yoshimura Namie Yomogida

Instructions: page 162

This festive eight-point star is made from diamonds accented with curved lines on a field of simple stars. The appliqué holiday border makes this quilt perfect for a child's bedroom.

Artists: Yoneko Arakaki Kyōko Katsumata Keiko Odanaka Setsuko Kobayashi Hiroko Sakai Kimiko Tamura Kyōko Fukushima Yoshiko Fujii Ryuko Minegishi

Star and Wreath Block

Star and Wreath Block (detail)

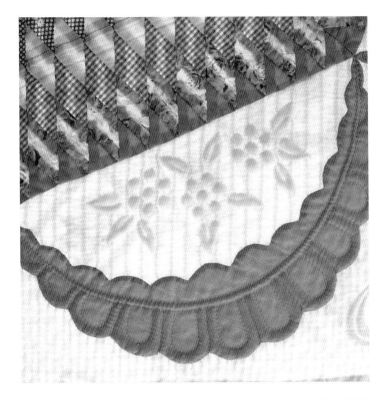

Instructions: page 150

Artist: Kazuko Ishii

Small stars ring the star in the center, which is expanded into a center medallion design. This is a delicate, elaborate design, overlaid on a beautiful trapunto quilt.

Larger Quilts

Sunburst

Diamonds radiate from the center star in this pattern, evoking the sun's rays. The bright color palette is as vibrant as the summer sun.

Artist: Yumiko Tanaka

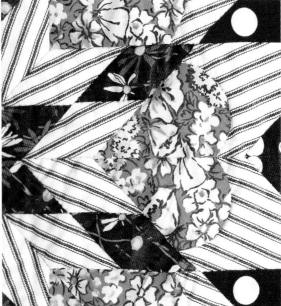

Instructions: page 148

Florida Star

Instructions: page 144

Artist: Momoe Miura

The Florida Star is a variation on the traditional pyramid quilt pattern (not featured in this book), which features continuous, linked triangles. Small stars are inset where the triangles meet—charming, hidden treasures.

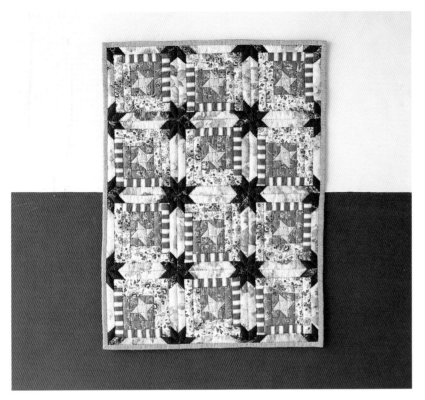

Mini-Quilts

Milky Way and Log Cabin

This design combines the traditional Log Cabin block with a Milky Way pattern. The two intertwined give order to the night sky.

Instructions: page 118

Artist: Keiko Odanaka

Mini-Quilts

Martha Washington Star

This 18th-century pattern was designed by the first First Lady of the United States, Martha Washington. Pinwheels appear to float in the center of the lone stars.

Instructions: page 120

Artist: Hisako Harasawa

Instructions: page 128

Artist: Nobuko Fukunaga

Displayed in a basket, the Star Flower resembles a sunflower. The diamond-studded frame and simple white field accentuate the floral arrangement.

Star Blossom

A lovely design, with stars placed in the
center of flower petals. Where the quilt block
corners align, a brilliant twin star appears.

Instructions: page 110

Artist: Tomoko Fujioka

Instructions: page 106

These stars are comprised of diamonds, stitched from various fabrics, which gives the pattern an all-around folk-art style.

Artist: Sakurako Kurihara

Mini Month-by-Month Quilt

This miniature quilt was made half the size of Month-by-Month
Quilt I (shown on the opposite page). Each piece has been reduced
equally in scale so the quilt blocks appear exactly the same.

Artist: Yutaka Ōtsuki

Instructions: page 139

Instructions: page 134

Month-by-Month Quilt I is a collection of eight-point stars fashioned from diamonds. Sew one of twelve unique star designs each month for one year to create the design.

Artists: Reiko Washizawa Yōko Asao

Month-by-Month Quilt II

Artists: Katsuko Akimoto Shizue Andō Kiyomi Ishikawa Kimiko Inagaki Masako Ōgawara Yōko Komazawa Yōko Takashiba Yumiko Tokunaga Kazuko Nakashima Toshiko Matsuo
Yōko Minegishi Yoshiko Yamagishi

Instructions: page 140

The shapes at play here are squares and circles, and the twelve unique star pattern blocks are unadorned at the seams and corners. It is a refreshing design with a tricolor palette of red, white, and blue.

Tote Bags

Lone Star (top)
Shooting Star II (bottom)

Small totes can be crafted from mini-quilts. Since they are just about half the size of a full-sized quilt, you can sew two minis in just about the same amount of time.

Instructions: page 188

Artist: Tae Kitagawa (top)
Artist: Yōko Asao (bottom)

Tote Bags

Milky Way and Log Cabin (top left)
Star Blossom (top right)
Stardust Memory (bottom)

Instructions: page 190

Artist: Suzuko Okada (top)
Artist: Setsuko Matsushita (middle)
Artist: Toshie Kitazume (bottom)

Eight-Point Star

Instructions: page 142

The simplest of the star patterns, the eight-point stars are arranged in the center with trapunto filled in between. The soft color palette evokes the barely visible, dim stars of the spring sky.

Artist: Reiko Washizawa

Wandering Diamond

This pattern is named after the meandering diamonds, which float like confetti with the cute stars.

Instructions: page 114

Artist: Yuko Okada

Instructions: page 186

Different-colored pouches are fashioned from the Wandering Diamond quilt (facing page).

Artist: Chisato Kuratani (top)
Artist: Fumiyo Hayakawa (bottom)

Feathered-Edge Star of Bethlehem

The Star of Bethlehem is outlined by a glittery rim. This quilt's color scheme is one part spring, one part springtime festival (Mardi Gras).

Feathered-Edge Star of Bethlehem (detail)

Instructions: page 158

Artists: Hiroko Ninagawa Chieko Kunimatsu

Tumbling Star

Instructions: page 160

This pattern's stars appear to roll and tumble about, each one gear-like and nearly in motion.

Artist: Hideko Mayuzumi

Pinwheel Star

This quilt block's center star seems to spin like a pinwheel in the breeze.

Instructions: page 132

Artist: Yoshiko Takahashi

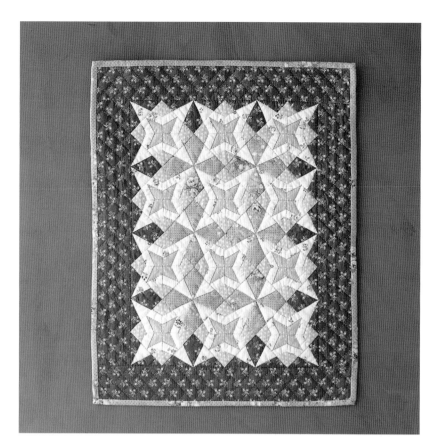

Mini-Quilts

Stardust Memory

When these four-point stars are aligned in a grid of twelve, their white outlines appear to glow.

Instructions: page 112

Artist: Yasuko Takeuchi

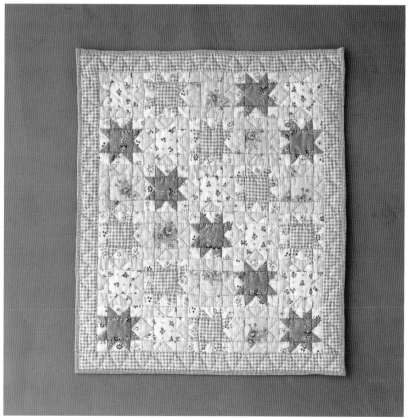

Mini-Quilts

Lone Star

These little stars tumble down the quilt block like sugar crystals. This is a basic pattern that can be made from four-patch blocks.

Instructions: page 108

Artist: Taeko Watanabe

Mini-Quilts

Shooting Star I

Instructions: page 116

This simple pattern is also known as a nine-patch star.

Artist: Masumi Yamashita

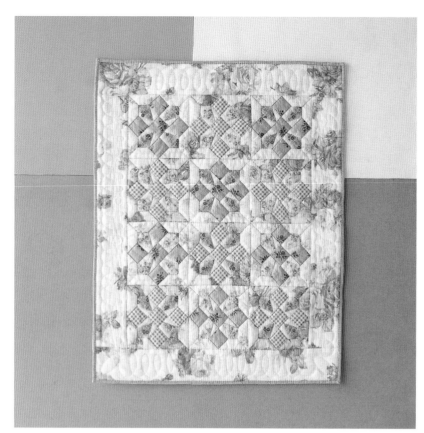

Mini-Quilts
Shooting Star II

A variation on the pattern shown at left. Diamonds are inset on four sides, evoking flower petals.

Instructions: page 122

Artist: Setsuko Ishii

Mini-Quilts
Spring Star

Tulips are arranged between the points of a Bethlehem Star. The image here is of a spring scene of blooming flowers.

Instructions: page 126

Artist: Kazuyo Fujita

Broken Star

This center star embellished with diamonds creates a
snowflake-like motif on a crisp, wintry blue background.
This winter star glows clear and bright in the night sky.

Instructions: page 124

Artist: Ritsuko Ariki

Feathered Star Tree

Instructions: page 130

This feathered star arrangement is like frosty evergeens on a field of snow—a perfect winter design.

Artist: Minae Murayama

Ten-Point Star

The Ten-Point Star is an original design of the artists.
This intricately pieced star radiates light from its dozens of facets.

Artists: Mayumi Hattori Rumiko Muraki

Instructions: page 154

Instructions: page 152

This is a modern quilt design with stacked squares and overlapping four-patch stars.
Around the center design, trapunto softens the bold, straight lines.

Artist: Yōko Kado

Part II

Materials, Techniques, and Patterns

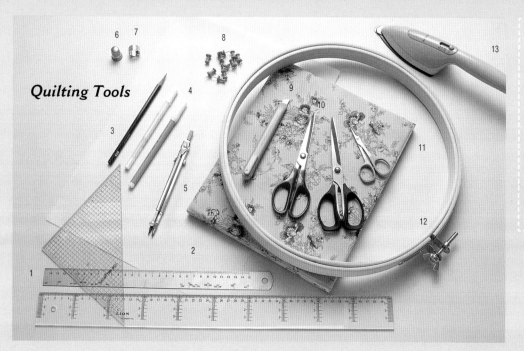

Quilting Tools

Sewing Tips

In the step photos, the word "mark" refers to the traced pattern line, which unless otherwise noted sits ¼" (6 mm) from the cut fabric edge.

When sewing from traced pattern line to traced pattern line (or mark to mark), use a backstitch at the beginning and the end.

When sewing from cut fabric edge to edge, do not use a backstitch.

1 Square ruler (for making paper patterns), a ruler, and a triangle (for transferring patterns onto fabric and drawing quilting lines).

2 Tracing paper (for making paper patterns)

3 Pencil (for making paper patterns)

4 Water-soluble markers

5 Compass (for drawing arcs and circles in paper patterns)

6 Thimble (for quilting)

7 Ring thimble

8 Thumbtacks (for securing fabric to a quilting or design board before quilting)

9 Craft knife (for making paper patterns)

10 Scissors (three styles, left to right: paper, cloth, and thread; use paper scissors for cutting quilt batting)

11 Patchwork board (one side is for cutting/marking, the other is a small ironing board)

12 Embroidery hoop (for quilting)

13 Iron (miniature model shown here)

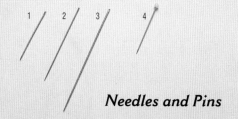

Needles and Pins

1 Hand-Sewing Needle (a short needle for quilting or stringing and sewing beads)

2 Appliqué Needle (a thin, medium-length needle for hemstitching appliqué and binding)

3 Basting/Tacking Needle (a long needle for sewing long basting stitches)

4 Quilting Pins (for securing fabric and marking seams before sewing or assembling a quilt)

Thread

In quilting, most thread (except basting) will be visible in the finished quilt, so always choose a matching or complementary color.

1 Appliqué Thread (very fine, nearly invisible; for appliqué)

2 Quilting Thread (heavy cotton thread; for quilting by hand)

3 Sewing Thread (for machine sewing)

4 Basting Thread (for temporary stitches)

Round-Robin Quilts

Five-Point Compass I & II

Quilts shown on pages 8 and 9

Finished size 36" × 36" (91.4 × 91.4 cm)

Patterns (see insert): side B

Units: inches (cm)

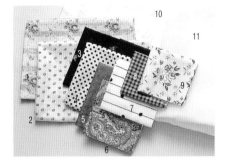

Materials

COTTON FABRIC

1	Unbleached Border (Pieces j·k·l·m·o·p·q·t·u , binding fabric)	43⁵⁄₁₆" × 7⅞" (110 × 20 cm)
2	Unbleached Small Flower Print (Pieces r·s·v·x·y, border ① ②)	43⁵⁄₁₆" × 47¼" (110 × 120 cm)
3	Red Small Flower Print (Pieces a·b·h·i·j·v, appliqué fabric)	43⁵⁄₁₆" × 19¹¹⁄₁₆" (110 × 50 cm)
4	Red Polka Dots (Pieces d–w)	25⅝" × 13¾" (65 × 35 cm)
5	Red Woven Print (Piece f)	17¾" × 5⅞" (45 × 15 cm)
6	Green Paisley (appliqué fabric)	13¾" × 14³⁄₁₆" (35 × 36 cm)
7	Ladybug Border (Pieces c–e)	13¾" × 3¹⁵⁄₁₆" (35 × 10 cm)
8	Red Checkerboard Print (Piece g)	13¾" × 7⅞" (35 × 20 cm)
9	Blue Flower Print (Piece n)	19¹¹⁄₁₆" × 11¹³⁄₁₆" (50 × 30 cm)
10	Pastel Flower Print (backing)	43⁵⁄₁₆" × 43⁵⁄₁₆" (110 × 110 cm)

BATTING

11	Batting	43⁵⁄₁₆" × 43⁵⁄₁₆" (110 × 110 cm)

Guide to Quilt Measurements

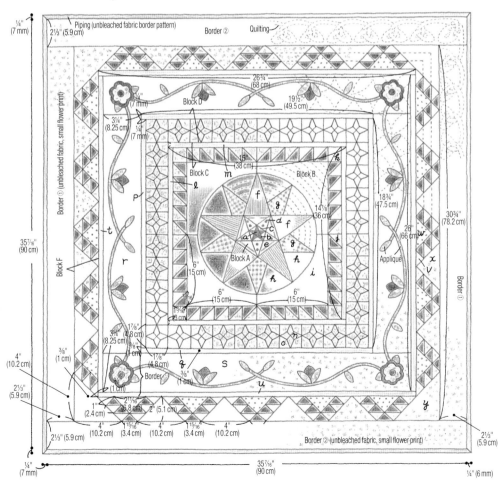

In the photos, contrasting threads are used to better illustrate stitches.

Finished measurements account for the slight shrinkage that occurs during quilting.

A–F are referred to as Blocks, and a–y are referred to as Pieces.

1 sheet each: Right Side Fabric (patchwork) (batting), Wrong Side Fabric (Print Pattern)

Cut along a ⅛" (3 mm) seam for small pieces, a ¼" (6 mm) seam for other pieces and borders, and a ¹⁄₁₆" (1.5 mm) seam for appliqué fabric.

Prepare 43⁵⁄₁₆" x 43⁵⁄₁₆" (110 × 110 cm) for the wrong-side fabric and quilt fabric.

1. Make Block A

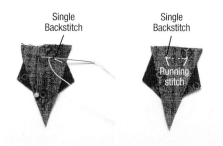

Mark Mark

Single Backstitch   Single Backstitch

Single Backstitch   Single Backstitch

Running stitch

1 Referring to the paper pattern, make the paper patterns for Pieces a-y, and cut each fabric piece with a ⅛"-¼" (3–6 mm) margin. Start by sewing together Pieces a and b.

2 Align the center of the right side of b with one side of a, then insert pins where marked.

3 Make a knot at the end of the thread, then insert the needle at the mark and make a single backstitch. Continue by making a running stitch along the sewing line, then make a single backstitch at the marking point. Finish with a quilter's knot and cut the thread.

Right Side   Wrong Side

4 Following Steps 2–3, sew together the other four b Pieces to the remaining sides of a. The seam allowance should fall to the b side.

5 Between the edges of Piece b, insert Piece c and sew together.

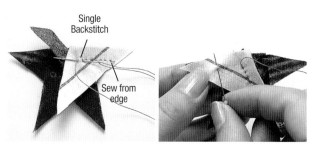

Single Backstitch

Sew from edge

Single Backstitch

Sew to mark

6 Center the right sides of b and c (on the o side), then sew from edge to the end of the traced line. At the end of the traced line, make a single backstitch, change directions, and insert a pin into the edge of the opposite side (on the x side).

7 At the end of the traced line make a backstitch, and then sew out to the edge.

8 Let the seam allowance fall to the c side, and turn over to the right side. In the same manner, sew together c Pieces along the remaining sides.

9 Cut off extra seam allowance.

10 Next, sew Pieces c and d together from mark point to mark point (the △ side). Let the seam allowance fall to the Piece d side.

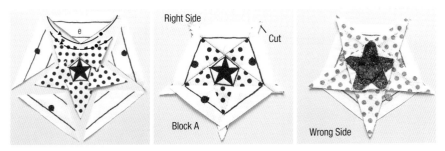

11 Fit Piece e into Piece d and sew together (the ● and ▲ sides from the ends of the traced lines). Let the seam allowance fall to the side of Piece e. Trim extra seam allowance. Block A is complete.

2. Sew Pieces f–i onto Block A, and complete Block B

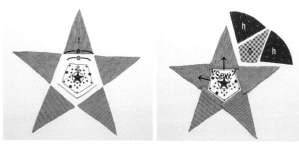 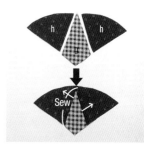 

1 Sew Piece f onto Piece e of Block A, from mark to mark (on the ◉ side). Allow the seam allowance to fall to the side of Piece f. Sew on the remaining four f Pieces in the same manner.

2 Make the Block that will fit into Piece f. Using an outline satin stitch, sew together Pieces g and h, letting the seam allowance fall to the side of Piece h. Make five of these Blocks.

3 Fit Block 2 pieces and sew together to Piece f (refer to steps 6–8 of Block A). Allow the seam allowance to fall to the side of the block.

4 Using an outline satin stitch, sew together the four i Pieces, letting the seam allowance fall to each side. Flip over to the wrong side, align the paper pattern, and copy the tracing lines. One piece of pattern paper can be used for both the right and wrong sides. Align it and copy the tracing lines.

Block B

5 Center Block 3 and Block 4, and insert marking pins at the tracing line. Sew together using a running stitch, and allow the seam allowances to fall to the outside. Press with an iron. Block B is complete.

3. Sew Pieces j–m to Block B, and finish Block C

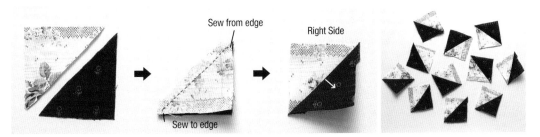

1 Cut out 40 pieces each of the unbleached border fabric and the red small flower print fabric. Sew a piece of the unbleached border fabric to a piece of the red small flower fabric, letting the seam allowance fall to the red side. Make 40 squares.

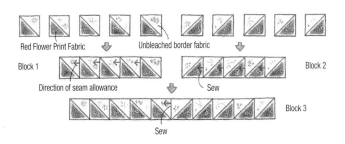

2 Join five of the square blocks and make Blocks 1 and 2. Join Blocks 1 and 2 as shown to form Block 3. Make four of Block 3.

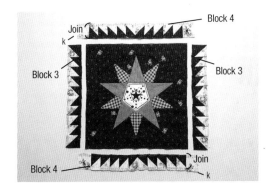

3 With two pieces of Block 3, sew on Piece k at each end to make Block 4. Make two, letting the seam allowance fall to one side.

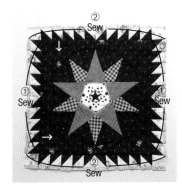

4 Using an outline satin stitch, sew Block 3 onto the left and right sides of Block B, then repeat at the top and bottom with Block 4. Let the seam allowance fall to the inside.

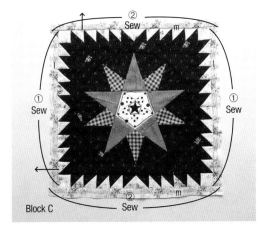

5 Using an outline satin stitch, attach Piece l to the right and left side of the four blocks, and Piece m to the top and bottom. Let the seam allowances fall to the outside. Block C is now complete.

4. Sew Pieces n–q to Block C, and complete Block D

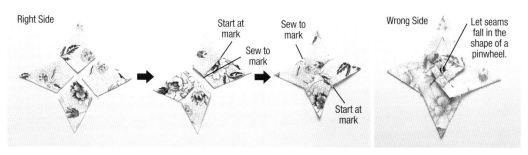

1 Cut out 144 of Piece n. Four pieces of n make up one star. To start, sew together two pieces side by side from mark to mark to form a block. Make a second block. Sew together these two blocks from mark to mark, letting the seam allowances fall in the shape of a pinwheel. Make 36.

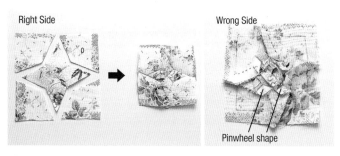

2 Fit in and sew Piece o onto one of the blocks to create a square block. Let the seam allowances fall into the shape of a pinwheel.

3 Using an outline satin stitch, sew together eight square blocks to form Block 6, and 10 square blocks to form Block 5. Make two each of Blocks 5 and 6. Let the seam allowance fall to one side.

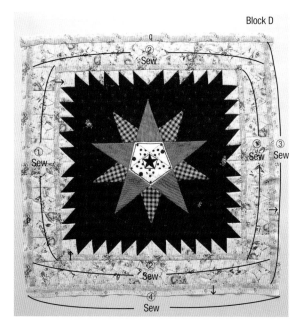

4 Using an outline satin stitch, sew Block 6 to the left and right sides, and Block 5 to the top and bottom of Block C. Let the seam allowance fall to the inside. Then use an outline satin stitch to sew Piece p to the left and right sides, and Piece q to the top and bottom. Let the seam allowance fall to the outside. Block D is now complete.

5. Sew Pieces r–u to Block D, creating Block E

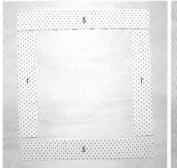
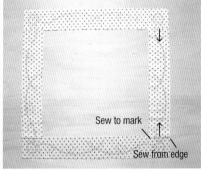

1 Cut out two pieces each of r and s from the unbleached small flower cloth and sew them together from edge to mark. Let the seam allowance fall to the side of Piece r. Copy the appliqué design using a marking pen.

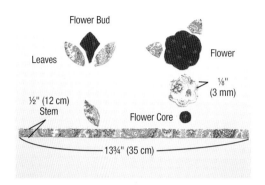

2 Copy the finished outline for the flower, bud, and leaf onto the right side of the appliqué fabric. Cut out shapes, adding a ⅛" (3 mm) seam allowance. Cut out 13¾" (35 cm) of the same fabric for the stem with a ½" (12 mm) bias, and then draw a ⅛" (3 mm) seam line on one side of the wrong side.

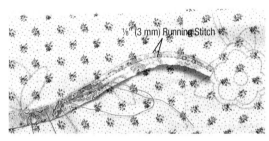

3 Create the appliqué stem. Align the outside of the appliqué design for the stem with the sewing line on the fabric, and then insert pins. The end of the stem should be ⅛" (3 mm) from the inside of the flower appliqué. Make a running stitch along the sewing line.

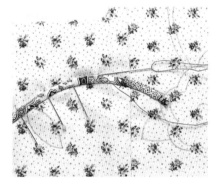

4 Turn the appliqué stem over to the right side, making three folds along the width of the stem. Sew with a vertical hemstitch. Make eight appliqué stems.

5 Make the appliqué leaves. Place each leaf onto the base fabric, and insert pins. Use the head of the pin to stuff the seam allowance inside, and sew to the tip of the leaf using a vertical hemstitch.

6 With the tip of the needle, fold and tuck the seam allowance at the leaf tip to the inside. The leaf tip should be sharp. Continue to stuff the seam allowance to the inside, and hemstitch towards the leaf base.

7 Do not hemstitch the leaf base, which overlaps the appliqué fabric. Hemstitch the second leaf the same way.

8 Make the appliqué flower base. Cut to the design edge at the V-shaped points in the seam allowance. While tucking the seam allowance to the inside, sew with a vertical hemstitch. Be sure to stitch once across the Vs.

9 Repeat step 8 for the flower top: cut into the seam allowance at the Vs, then sew it onto the base using a vertical hemstitch.

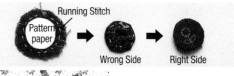

10 Make the flower center. Sew a running stitch along the seam allowance, leaving a short thread tail at the end without closing it. Insert the pattern paper and cinch the thread. Press with an iron and shape the piece properly. Remove the paper pattern and again form the shape, balling it up. Align the piece on top of the flower and sew around it using a vertical hemstitch.

11 Next, make the appliqué flower buds, which run along the quilt edges.

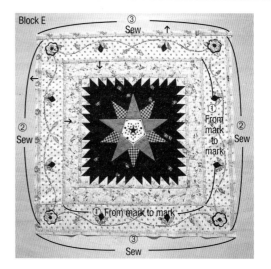

12 Fit the block from step 11 around Block D, and sew from mark to mark, pulling together the four sides. Let the seam allowance fall to the side of Block D. Sew on Piece t to the left and right, and Piece u to the top and bottom using an outline satin stitch. Let the seam allowance fall to the outside. Block E is now complete.

6. Sew Pieces v–y to Block E and make Block F

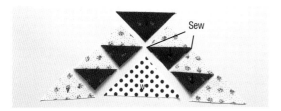

1 Using an outline satin stitch, sew together Piece v of the red small flower print fabric and the unbleached small flower print fabric to make 80 square blocks.

2 After you have sewn together two of the square blocks each from step 1 using an outline satin stitch, sew on Piece v of the unbleached small flower print fabric to the bottom of the right-hand side, and a Piece v of each type of fabric to the top and bottom of the left-hand side, using an outline satin stitch. Let the seam allowance fall to the side of the red small flower print fabric.

3 Sew the right-hand side block from step 2 to the right-hand side of Piece w using an outline satin stitch, letting the seam allowance fall to the side of Piece w.

4 On the other side of Piece w, sew the left-hand side block from step 2 using an outline satin stitch, and let the seam allowance fall to the side of Piece w. Make 20 blocks.

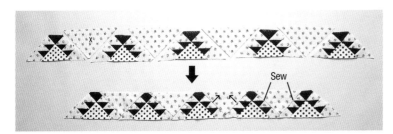

5 Alternate five of the triangular blocks from step 4 with four of Piece x, and sew together using an outline satin stitch. Let the seam allowance fall to the side of Piece x. Make four blocks.

6 Sew the blocks from step 5 one by one to the edges of Block E using an outline satin stitch, and let the seam allowance fall to the side of Block E. Sew Piece y to the four corners using an outline satin stitch, and let the seam allowance fall to the side of Piece y. Block F is complete.

7. Sew on the border and complete the top

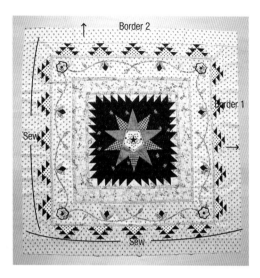

Using an outline satin stitch, sew Border 1 to the left and right side of Block F, and Border 2 to the top and bottom. Let the seam allowance fall to the side of the borders. Press with an iron to flatten out the entire piece. The quilt top is complete.

8. Draw the quilting lines

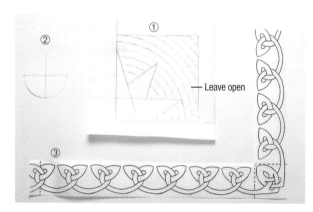

1 Use thick tracing paper to make the paper pattern that you will use to copy the quilting lines. Pattern ① is ¼ of the pattern to copy the curved lines onto Blocks A and B. Make holes in the dotted line of the curves. Pattern ② is a 3¹/₁₆" (8 cm) circle for drawing the wine glass design. Add vertical and horizontal centering lines. ③ is the border design. Make sure to note centering and squaring marks.

2 Align paper pattern ① in the A•B Block position of the quilt top, and using a marking pen, trace the dotted line with the holes. Remove the pattern paper and connect the dotted lines to make solid lines. Use the front and the back of the pattern paper and make solid lines all around.

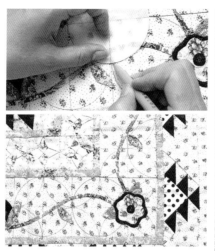

3 Draw lines at 3¼ " (8.25 cm) intervals around the appliqué area of Block E. Next, halfway across, draw vertical and horizontal lines. At the intersection of these lines, align paper pattern ② and draw circles.

4 While shifting the pattern paper over a half circle at a time, copy the outline and complete the wine glass design.

5 Align the corner of pattern ③ and place on top of the border of the quilt top. Copy the design. While shifting the pattern paper, copy the design over the entire border.

Quilting Design

9. Baste and Quilt

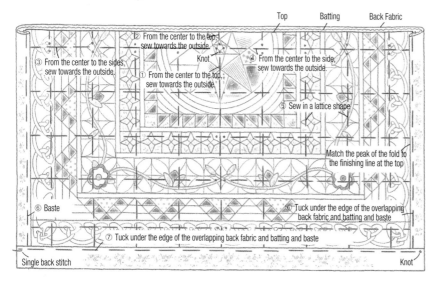

Top Batting Back Fabric

② From the center to the top, sew towards the outside.

Knot

③ From the center to the sides, sew towards the outside.

④ From the center to the side, sew towards the outside.

① From the center to the top, sew towards the outside.

⑤ Sew in a lattice shape

Match the peak of the fold to the finishing line at the top

⑥ Baste

⑥ Tuck under the edge of the overlapping back fabric and batting and baste

⑦ Tuck under the edge of the overlapping back fabric and batting and baste

Single back stitch

Knot

1 On a flat board, spread out the back fabric, wrong side up. Secure the four corners with thumbtacks. Layer the quilt batting and the quilt top piece, making sure to align and center each layer. Pin layers in place with thumbtacks. From the center to the sides and top, baste in a lattice shape. Tuck under the edge of the overlapping back fabric and batting and baste. (See diagram.)

2 Set up the embroidery hoop. Layer the quilt center on top of the inner ring of the hoop. Then fit the outer ring around the inner ring, from the top. Adjust the tension of the quilt so it is taut for hand sewing, then tightly fasten the screw.

The Quilting Process

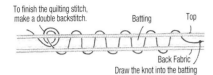

To finish the quilting stitch, make a double backstitch.

Batting Top

Back Fabric
Draw the knot into the batting

3 To begin quilting: Use red thread for the red sections of Block B, and unbleached quilting thread for all other areas. Put a thimble on the middle finger of your sewing hand. Start with the running stitch on Block A. Quilting is worked from the center of the quilt outward. When you have completed the section within the hoop, reposition and tighten the hoop over the next section to be done, and continue quilting. In quilting, a running stitch (also called rocking stitch) is also added along the edges of each piece and appliqué.

Start the Quilting

Knot

1 Make a knot at the end of a long piece of thread and feed the other end into the needle. Pass the needle through the batting and pull out where the stitch line begins. Tug the thread and pull the knot to the inside.

2 Insert the needle back into the stitch position, and make a shallow running stitch, scooping the batting and back fabric with the needle tip. The running stitch runs along the edge of the piece.

Finish the Quilting Stitch

1 On the last stitch, scoop the needle through only to the batting and make a single backstitch.

Exit

2 Insert the needle once more into the same spot as in step 1, draw the needle through the batting, and make a long stitch. Tug the thread and cut it at the edge of the fabric.

4 Trim the extra quilt batting and backing and align with the quilt top edges.

10. Bind and Finish

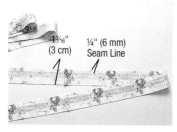

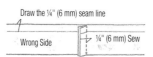

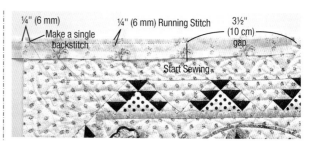

1³⁄₁₆" (3 cm) ¼" (6 mm) Seam Line

Creating the binding

Draw the ¼" (6 mm) seam line

Wrong Side   ¼" (6 mm) Sew

1 Cut a 1¼" (3 cm) wide strip of the unbleached border fabric, 4.4 yd (400 cm) long. Draw a ¼" (6 mm) seam allowance along the inside of the edge.

¼" (6 mm) Make a single backstitch   ¼" (6 mm) Running Stitch   3½" (10 cm) gap   Start Sewing

2 Align the finishing line (of quilting) of the main body with the binding seam allowance, and pin in place. Start sewing from about 3½" (10 cm) inside the edge of the binding fabric. Scooping the needle through to the quilt backing, make a running stitch up to a point that is ¼" (6 mm) inside the corner. Make a single backstitch in the corner.

Align the curve of the fold to the top edge.   ¼" (6 mm) Running Stitch

Binding Fabric (Wrong Side)

3 Fold the binding fabric into right angles.

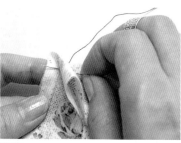

Make a single backstitch

4 Insert the needle at the corner of the binding fabric (allowing the needle to pass through only the binding fabric), then pull the needle through from the opposite corner. Make a single backstitch in the corner (scooping the main body fabric with the needle), then make a running stitch to the next corner.

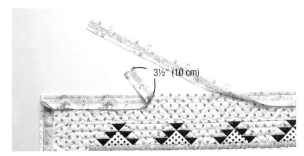

3½" (10 cm)

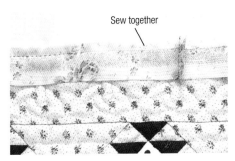

Sew together

5 Repeat steps 2–4, and sew to 3½" (10 cm). Sew from the edge of the first piece of binding fabric you started with. When you have created binding all around the quilt and you are sewing the last piece of binding fabric, leave a ¼" (6 mm) seam allowance. This is where you will join the first and last strips of binding, then cut off the extra.

6 Using a running stitch, sew together the edges of the binding fabric at the ¼" (6 mm) seam allowance. Let the seam allowance fall to one side.

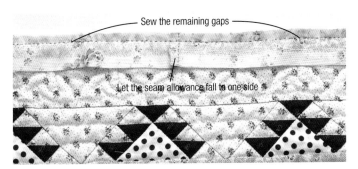

Sew the remaining gaps

Let the seam allowance fall to one side

7 Line up the binding fabric from step 6 with the main body and sew the remaining gaps.

Wrong Side

8 Wrap the seam allowance with the binding fabric (triple folded), and insert pins. The corners fold up into a frame. With the tip of the needle, scoop the edge of the seam through to the batting and make a vertical hem stitch. Do not sew the frame corners.

9 Launder the quilt in water with a mild detergent to remove the marking pen. Rinse well with water to ensure all the detergent is removed. Roll it up with a towel to draw out any extra moisture. Re-shape the quilt and hang it to dry on a rack out of direct sunlight. The quilt is now finished.

Here we will introduce the methods used for sewing 14 styles of stars. The basics of sewing a star pattern are the same for all 14 styles. Once you have mastered these methods, you can use them as a reference when you are creating new patterns and motifs.

Leave a ⅛" (3 mm) seam allowance for the smaller main pieces and a ¼" (6 mm) allowance for the larger pieces. Cut the appliqué fabric with a 1/16" (1.5 mm) seam allowance.

Pieces a and a' are made with the same paper pattern, but in reverse. Make a paper pattern for each shape so there is no confusion when cutting the fabric.

PATTERN 1.

Hexagon Star

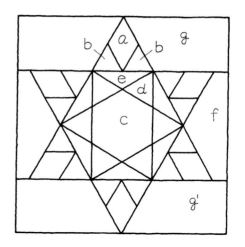

As seen in the Feathered Star round-robin quilt, page 10

1 Sew together Pieces a and b using an outline satin stitch, letting the seam allowance fall to the side of Piece b. Make six blocks.

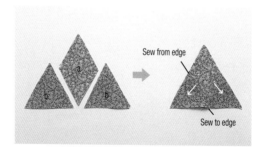

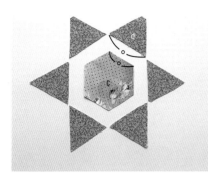

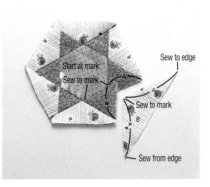

2 Sewing from mark to mark, attach Piece d to the six sides of Piece c (○). Next, join the (×) sides of Pieces d and e, sewing from edge to mark. Make a single backstitch at the point of the mark, then turn the fabric to align the (△) and insert pins. Again, make a backstitch at the marking point and sew together towards the edge (fitting it in as you go along). Let the seam allowances fall into the shape of a pinwheel.

3 Sewing from mark to mark, join Piece e and the blocks made in step 1.

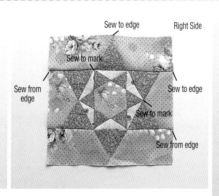

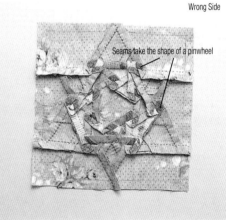

4 Fit Piece f into the left and right side of the block from step 3 and sew together. Pieces g and g' can also be sewn in the same manner. Let the seam allowance fall into the shape of a pinwheel. The pattern is complete.

PATTERN 2.

Ohio Star

As seen in the Ohio Star round-robin quilt, page 19

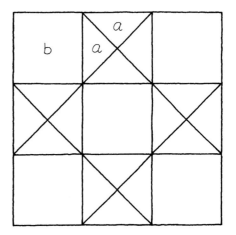

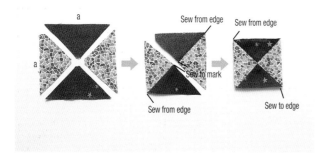

1 Arrange the a Pieces of the dark blue fabric and the a Pieces of the blue fabric as shown. Sew together, working from edge towards the mark. Sew these two blocks together from edge to edge, and make a square block. Allow the seam allowances to take the shape of a pinwheel at the center.

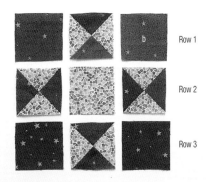

Row 1

Row 2

Row 3

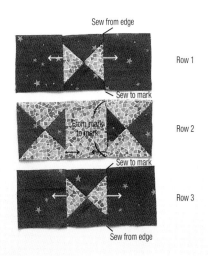

Sew from edge

Row 1

Sew to mark

From mark to mark

Row 2

Sew to mark

Row 3

Sew from edge

2 Make four square blocks from step 1. Cut out four b Pieces from the dark blue fabric and one from the blue fabric. Alternately arrange the b Pieces with the blocks, and align the three Rows.

3 Sew each of the blocks of the three Rows together. For Rows 1 and 3, sew from edge to mark. For Row 2, sew from mark to mark.

Right Side

Wrong Side

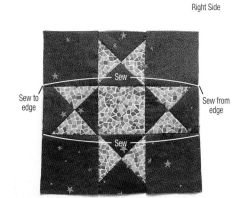

Sew to edge

Sew

Sew from edge

Sew

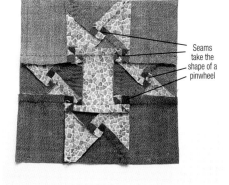

Seams take the shape of a pinwheel

Paper Pattern Guide

Cut pieces with a ¼" (6 mm) seam allowance.

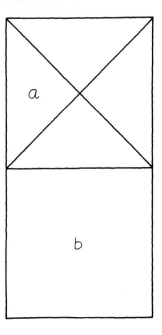

a

b

4 Sew together the Row 1 and Row 2 blocks from step 3, working from edge to edge. Next, sew together the Row 2 and Row 3 blocks in the same way. Let the seam allowances fall into the shape of a pinwheel. The pattern is complete.

PATTERN 3.

Rosebud

As seen in the Eternal Blossom round-robin quilt, page 16

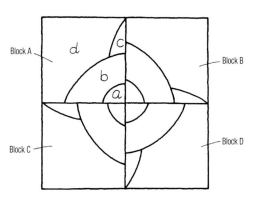

1 Make Block A. Align the center of the right sides of Pieces a and b. Insert marking pins. Sew together using an outline satin stitch, and let the seam allowance fall to the side of Piece a.

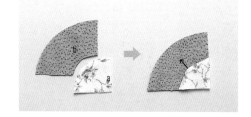

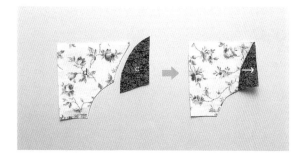

2 Using an outline satin stitch, sew together Pieces c and d, letting the seam allowance fall to the side of Piece c.

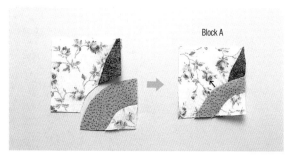

3 Using an outline satin stitch, sew together the Blocks from steps 1 and 2. Let the seam allowance fall toward the step 1 Block. Block A is complete.

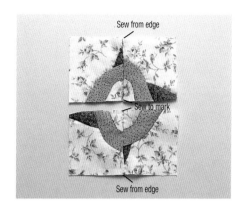

4 Make Blocks B, C, and D following the instructions in steps 1–3.

5 Working from the edge to the mark, sew together Blocks A and B. Sew Blocks C and D together in the same manner, then align the two blocks.

6 Working from edge to edge, sew together the two blocks from step 5. Let the seam allowance fall into the shape of a pinwheel. The pattern is now complete.

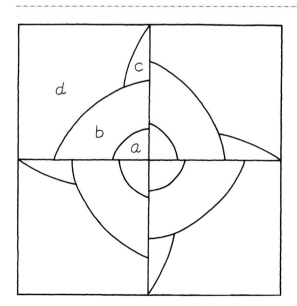

Paper Pattern Guide

For the small pieces, leave a ⅛" (3 mm) seam allowance. For all others leave a ¼" (6 mm) allowance.

PATTERN 4.

Scrap Star

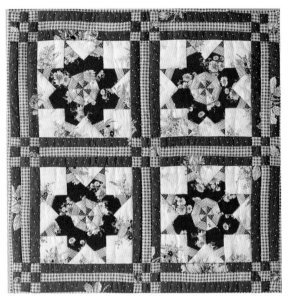

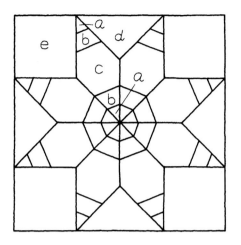

As seen in the Scrap Star mini-quilt, page 35

Block A

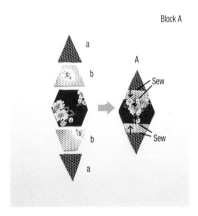

1 Sew Block A (use the green flower print fabric for Piece a). Using an outline satin stitch, sew Pieces a and b as shown. Let the seam allowance fall to the inside. Make four Block As.

Block B

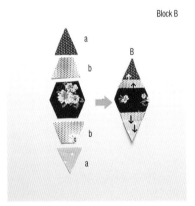

2 Sew Block B (use the yellow fabric for Piece a). Using an outline satin stitch, sew Pieces a and b as shown in step 1, letting the seam allowance fall to the outside. Make four Block Bs.

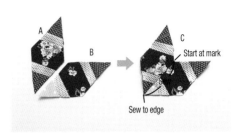

3 Sew together Blocks A and B. Sew from the mark to the edge, making Block C. Make four Block Cs.

4 Sewing from mark to mark, join two Block Cs to make Block D. Make one more block in the same manner.

5 Sewing from mark to mark, join the two Block Ds. Let the seam allowances in the middle fall into the shape of a pinwheel.

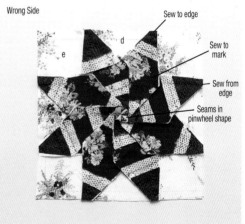

6 Fit Pieces d and e into the block from step 5, and sew together. Let the seam allowances fall toward the side of Pieces d and e. The pattern is complete.

PATTERN 5.

Lone Star

As seen in the Lone Star quilt, page 21

*As seen in the Lone Star bag,
page 40*

As seen in the Lone Star mini-quilt, page 51

As seen in the Martha Washington Star mini-quilt, page 32

1 Using a satin stitch, sew together Pieces a and b, letting the seam allowance fall to the side of Piece b. Make four rectangular blocks.

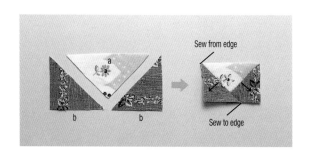

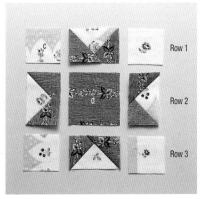

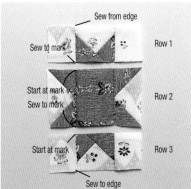

2 Align the blocks into three Rows. For Row 1 and Row 3, sew Piece c to both sides of one of the rectangular blocks from step 1, working from edge to mark. For Row 2, sew the rectangular blocks from step 1 to both sides of Piece d, working from mark to mark.

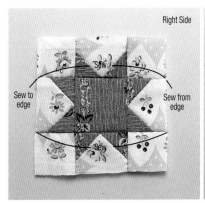

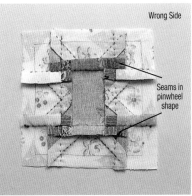

3 Sew together Row 1 and Row 2, working from edge to edge. Next, sew together Row 2 and Row 3, working from edge to edge. Let the seam allowance at each corner fall into the shape of a pinwheel.

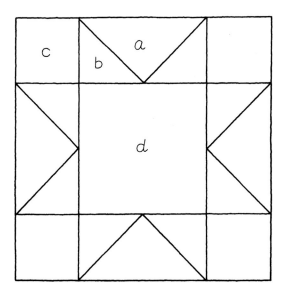

Paper Pattern Guide

Cut out the pieces leaving a ¼" (6 mm) seam allowance.

PATTERN 6.

Star Blossom

As seen in the Star Blossom
mini-quilt, page 34

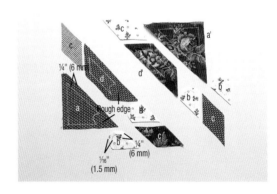

As seen in the Star Blossom
tote bag, page 41

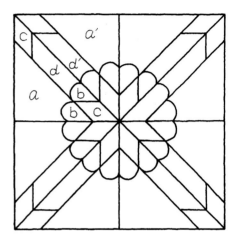

---

1 Since Pieces a, b, d, a', and d' are for appliqué, draw finishing lines and cut out leaving a ⅛" (3 mm) seam allowance. For the parts where the appliqué fabric layers overlap (see Pieces a, d, a', and d'), leave the edges rough and wider. Once you have sewn the appliqué, trim it into a ⅛" (3 mm) seam allowance. For the parts that will be pieced, leave a ¼" (6 mm) seam allowance.

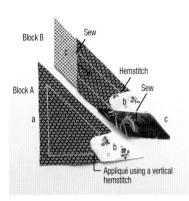

Block B
Sew
b
Block A
Hemstitch
Sew
a
b
c
b
Appliqué using a vertical hemstitch

2 Make Block A. Align Piece b along the curved sewing line on Piece a, then sew together using a vertical hemstitch, while tucking the seam allowance for the curved section to the inside using the tip of the needle. Make Block B. Appliqué Piece b to Piece d, then sew together Pieces c and d, and Pieces c and b with an outline satin stitch, letting the seam allowance fall to one side.

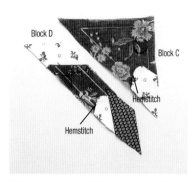

Block D
Block C
Hemstitch
Hemstitch

3 Sew together Blocks C and D in the same manner as Blocks A and B from step 2.

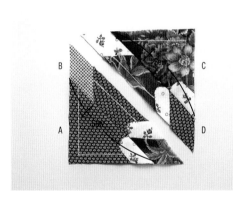

B
C
A
D

4 Using an outline satin stitch, sew together each of the Block As to Block Bs, and the Block Cs to the Block Ds. Let the seam allowances fall to one side. Next, sew the two blocks together using an outline satin stitch. Make four blocks.

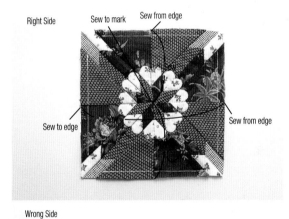

Right Side
Sew to mark
Sew from edge
Sew to edge
Sew from edge

Wrong Side

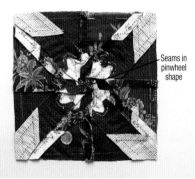

Seams in pinwheel shape

5 Align the four blocks as shown, so the star pattern appears in the center. Working from edge to mark, sew together two of the blocks along the side, making two new blocks. Sew these two new blocks together using an outline satin stitch. Let the seam allowances fall into the shape of a pinwheel. The pattern is now complete.

Part II. Materials, Techniques, and Patterns   87

PATTERN 7.

Stardust Memory

As seen in the Stardust Memory mini-quilt, page 51

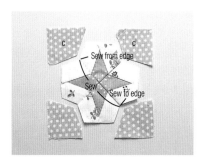

As seen in the Stardust Memory tote bag, page 41

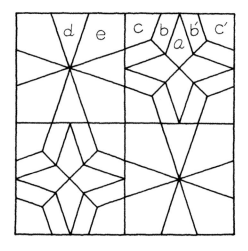

---

1 Make Pattern A. Sew Pieces b and b' to the left and right sides of Piece a using an outline satin stitch, and let the seam allowances fall towards the side of Pieces b and b'. Make four of these blocks.

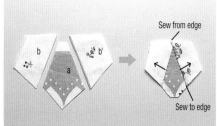

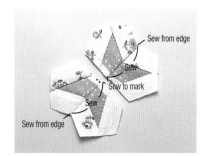

2 Sew together two of the blocks from step 1, working from edge to mark. Make two blocks.

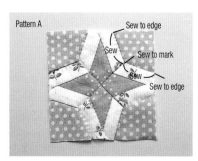

3 Sew together the two blocks from Step 2, working from edge to edge. Let the seam allowance fall into the shape of a pinwheel.

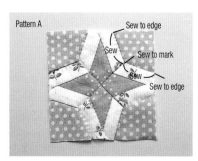

4 Fit Pieces c and c' into the block from step 3 and then sew together. Let the seam allowances fall into the shape of a pinwheel. Make two of Pattern A.

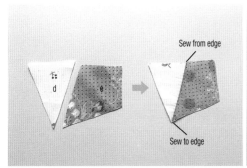

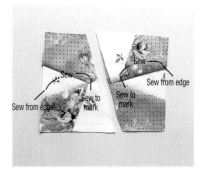

5 Make Pattern B. Sew together Pieces d and e using an outline satin stitch. Make four blocks.

6 Sew together the two blocks from step 5, working from edge to mark. Make two blocks.

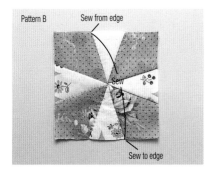

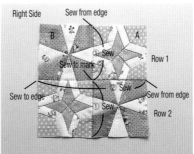

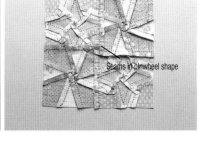

7 Sew together the two blocks from Step 6, letting the seam allowances fall into the shape of a pinwheel. Make two of Pattern B.

8 For Row 1, align Pattern B with A. For Row 2, align Pattern A with B. Sew each together from edge to mark, making two blocks. Sew these two blocks together from edge to edge. Let the seam allowances fall into the shape of a pinwheel. The pattern is now complete.

PATTERN 8.

Wandering Diamond

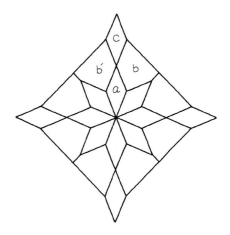

As seen in the Wandering Diamond mini-quilt, page 44

As seen in the Wandering Diamond small tote, page 45

1 From mark to edge, sew a Pieces together, one in flower print fabric and one in checkered fabric. Make four blocks.

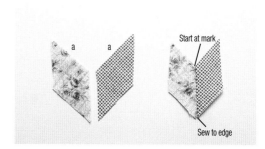

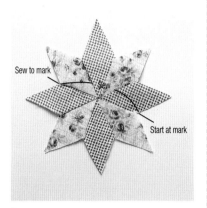

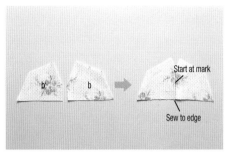

2 Sew together two of the blocks from step 1, working from mark to mark. Make two blocks.

3 Working from mark to mark, sew together the two blocks from step 2 to create the Star Block. Let the seam allowances fall into the shape of a pinwheel.

4 Sew together Pieces b and b' from the mark to the edge. Make four blocks.

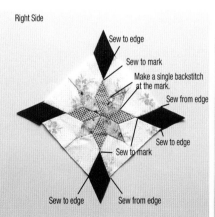

5 Fit the blocks from step 4 into the block from step 3 and sew together. Once all four are sewn on, insert c Pieces and sew together. Let the seam allowances fall into a pinwheel shape. The pattern is complete.

PATTERN 9.

Shooting Star II

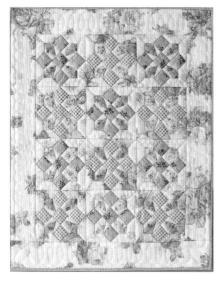

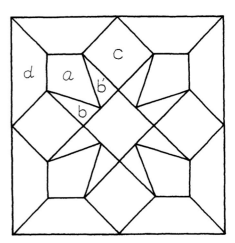

*As seen in the Shooting Star II
mini-quilt, page 53*

*As seen in the Shooting Star II
tote bag, page 40*

---

1 Using an outline satin stitch, sew Pieces b and b' to each side of Piece a, letting the seam allowance fall to the side of Pieces b and b'. Make four blocks.

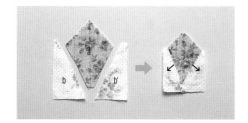

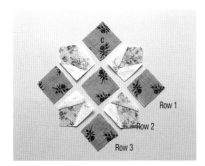

2 Align the blocks in three Rows, alternating the blocks from step 1 with Pieces c.

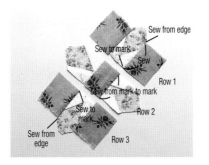

3 Sew together each Row, creating three Row Blocks. For Row 1 and Row 3, sew from edge to mark, and for Row 2 sew from mark to mark.

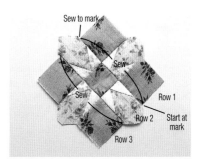

4 Working from mark to mark, sew together Rows 1–Row 3. Let the seam allowances fall into the shape of a pinwheel.

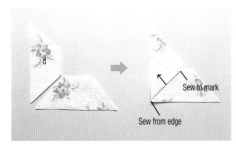

5 Sew together two d Pieces from edge to mark, letting the seam allowance fall to one side. Make four blocks.

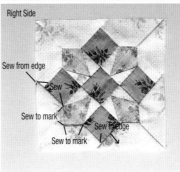

6 Place the four blocks from step 5 around the block from step 4 and sew together. Let the seam allowance fall to the outside. The pattern is complete.

Milky Way and Log Cabin

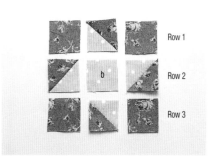

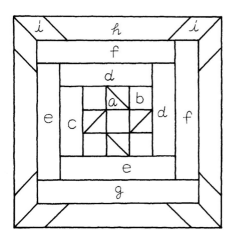

As seen in the Milky Way and Log Cabin mini-quilt, page 32

As seen in the Milky Way and Log Cabin tote bag, page 41

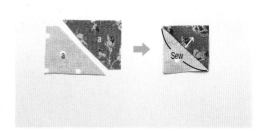

1 Sew together two a Pieces, one in the yellow print and one in the brown print, making a square block. Let the seam allowance fall toward the brown fabric. Make four blocks.

2 Arrange b Pieces and the square blocks from Step 1 into three Rows as shown.

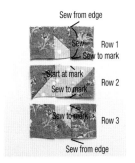

Sew from edge

Sew — Sew — Row 1
Sew to mark

Start at mark — Row 2
Sew to mark

Sew to mark — Row 3

Sew from edge

3 Sew together each Row, making three Row Blocks. For Row 1 and Row 3, sew from edge to mark, and for Row 2 sew from mark to mark.

Sew

Start at mark — Sew to mark

Sew

4 Working from mark to mark, sew together the three Row Blocks from step 3, letting the seam allowance fall into the shape of a pinwheel. The center block is complete.

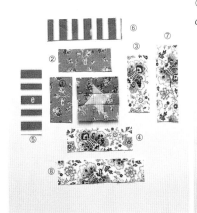

①–⑧ *refers to the order of the piecework.*

5 Sew Pieces c–g to the center block in numeric order as shown using an outline satin stitch. Let the seam allowances fall to the outside.

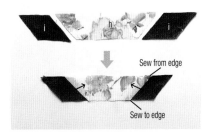

Sew from edge

Sew to edge

6 Sew Pieces i to both sides of Piece h, working from edge to edge. Let the seam allowance fall to the side of Piece h. Make four of the same block.

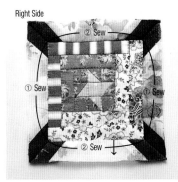

Right Side

② Sew

① Sew — ① Sew

② Sew

Wrong Side

7 Sew the step 6 blocks to the left and right side of the step 5 block, working from mark to mark. Next, fit the remaining step 6 blocks to the top and bottom and sew together. Let the seam allowances fall to the outside. The pattern is complete.

PATTERN 11.

Martha Washington Star

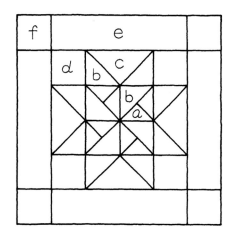

As seen in the Martha Washington Star mini-quilt, page 32

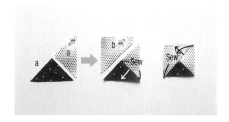

1 Make Block A. Using an outline satin stitch, sew together Piece a in dark green print and Piece a of the dotted print. Let the seam allowance fall to the dark green side. Next, sew on Piece b using an outline satin stitch, and let the seam allowance fall to the side of Piece b. Make four square blocks.

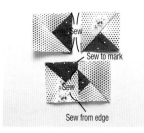

2 Align the four square blocks from step 1 as shown. Sew two together side by side, working from edge to mark. Make two blocks.

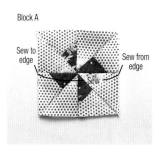

3 Sew together the two blocks from step 2 using an outline satin stitch. Let the seam allowances fall into the shape of a pinwheel. Block A is complete.

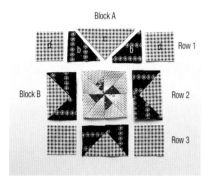

Block A

Row 1

Block B   Row 2

Row 3

4 Make Block B. Sew Piece b onto both sides of Piece c using an outline satin stitch, letting the seam allowance fall to the side of Piece b. Make four blocks, then align them in three Rows as shown.

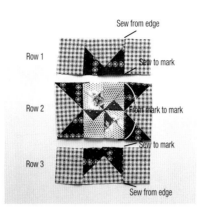

Sew from edge

Row 1   Sew to mark

Row 2   From mark to mark

Sew to mark

Row 3

Sew from edge

5 Make the Row 1 and Row 3 Blocks. Working from edge to mark, sew Pieces d to both sides of Block B. Next, make the Row 2 Block. Working from mark to mark, sew Blocks B to both sides of Block A.

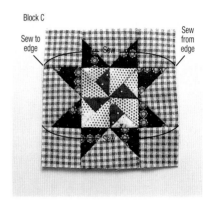

Block C

Sew to edge   Sew from edge

Sew

Sew

6 Sew together the three Row Blocks from step 5, working from edge to edge. Let the seam allowances fall into the shape of a pinwheel. Block C is complete.

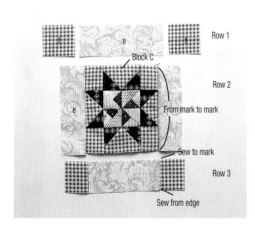

e   f   Row 1

Block C

Row 2

e   From mark to mark

Sew to mark

Row 3

Sew from edge

7 Complete the pattern. For the Row 1 and Row 3 Blocks, sew f Pieces onto both sides of Piece e, working from edge to mark. For the Row 2 Block, sew Pieces e onto both sides of Block C, working from mark to mark.

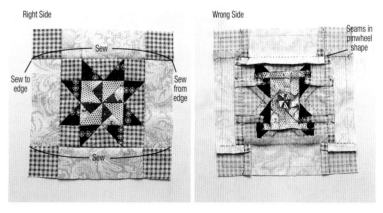

Right Side   Wrong Side

Sew   Seams in pinwheel shape

Sew to edge   Sew from edge

Sew

8 Sew together Row 1–3 Blocks, working from edge to edge. Let the seam allowances fall into the shape of a pinwheel. The pattern is complete.

PATTERN 12.

Tulip

As seen in the Morning Star
round-robin quilt, page 23

As seen in the Spring Star
mini-quilt, page 52

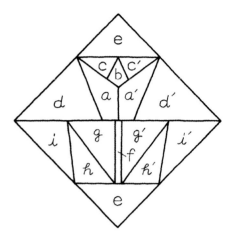

---

1 Make the Flower Block. Sew together Piece a and Piece a', working from edge to mark, and let the seam allowance fall to one side. Next, sew Piece c and Piece c' to both sides of Piece b using an outline satin stitch. Let the seam allowances fall to the sides of Piece c and c'.

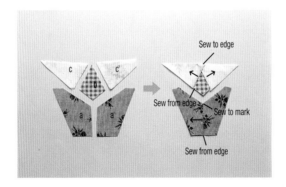

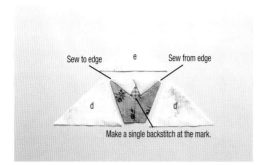

2 Fit and sew together the two blocks from step 1.

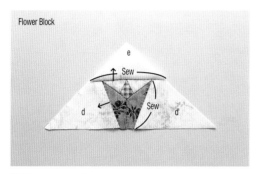

Flower Block

3 Using an outline satin stitch, sew Piece d and Piece d' to the left and right side of the block from step 2, letting the seam allowance fall to the side of Piece d and Piece d'. Next, sew Piece e to the top using an outline satin stitch, letting the seam allowance fall to the side of Piece e. The Flower Block is complete.

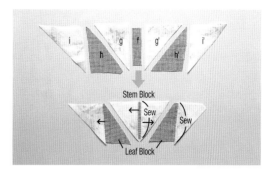

4 Make the Stem and Leaf Blocks. Sew Piece g and g' to both sides of Piece f using an outline satin stitch, letting the seam allowances fall to the sides of Pieces g and g'. Next, sew together Piece h (h') and Piece i (i') using an outline satin stitch. Let the seam allowance fall to the sides of Pieces i (i').

5 Sew the Leaf Blocks to both sides of the center Stem Block using an outline satin stitch. Let the seam allowances fall to the side of the Leaf Blocks. Sew Piece e to the bottom using an outline satin stitch, letting the seam allowance fall to the side of Piece e. The Stem and Leaf Block is complete.

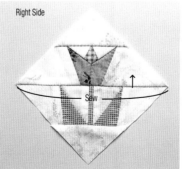

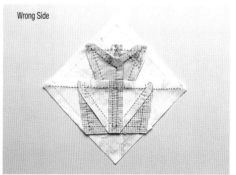

6 Using an outline satin stitch, sew together the Flower Block and the Stem and Leaf Block. Let the seam allowance fall to the side of the flower block. The pattern is complete.

PATTERN 13.

Pinwheel Star

As seen in the Pinwheel Star round-robin quilt, page 17

As seen in the Pinwheel Star mini-quilt, page 50

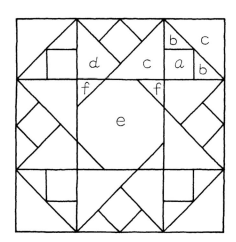

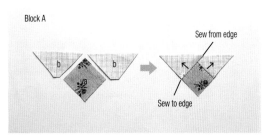

Block A

Sew from edge

Sew to edge

1 Using an outline satin stitch, sew b Pieces to both sides of Piece a, letting the seam allowance fall to the side of Piece b. Make eight Block As.

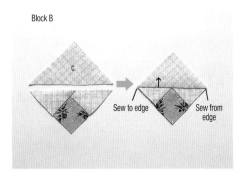

Block B

Sew to edge

Sew from edge

2 Make Block B. Sew Piece c to Block A using an outline satin stitch, and let the seam allowance fall to the side of Piece c. Make four blocks.

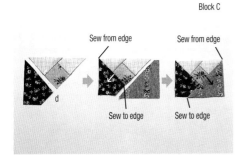

Block C

Sew from edge

Sew from edge

Sew to edge

Sew to edge

d

3 Make Block C. Using an outline satin stitch, sew Piece d to Block A and let the seam allowance fall to the side of Piece d. Next, using an outline satin stitch, sew on Piece c and let the seam allowance fall to the side of Piece c. Make four blocks.

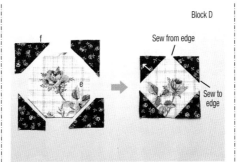

Block D

f

e

Sew from edge

Sew to edge

4 Make Block D. Using an outline stitch, sew four of Piece f to Piece e. Let the seam allowances fall to the side of Piece f.

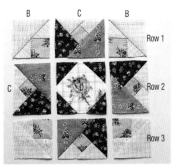

B   C   B

Row 1

C   D

Row 2

Row 3

5 Align Blocks B, C, and D as shown. Pay attention to the orientation of the Blocks.

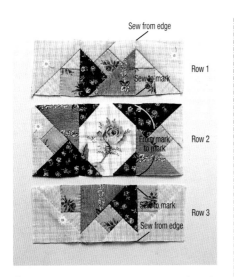

Sew from edge

Row 1

Sew to mark

From mark to mark

Row 2

Sew to mark

Sew from edge

Row 3

6 For Row 1 and Row 3, sew together the three blocks, working from edge to mark. For Row 2, sew from mark to mark.

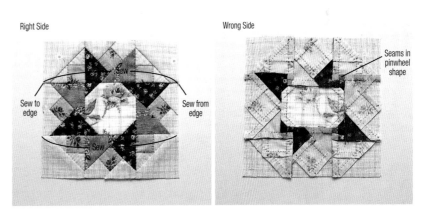

Right Side

Wrong Side

Sew

Sew to edge

Sew from edge

Sew

Seams in pinwheel shape

7 Sew together the three Row Blocks, working from edge to edge. Let the seam allowances fall into the shape of a pinwheel. The pattern is complete.

PATTERN 14.

Florida Star

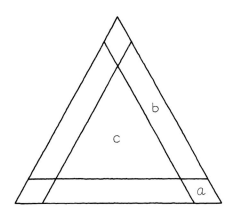

As seen in the Florida Star quilt, page 30

---

1 Make Block A. Using an outline satin stitch, sew Piece a onto both sides of Piece b, letting the seam allowance fall to the side of Piece b. Make Block B. Using an outline satin stitch, sew Piece a onto one side of Piece b, and let the seam allowance fall to the side of Piece b. Using an outline satin stitch, sew on Piece b and Blocks A and B in order ① – ③ to the center Piece c. Let the seam allowance fall to the outside. Make eight triangle blocks in varied color schemes.

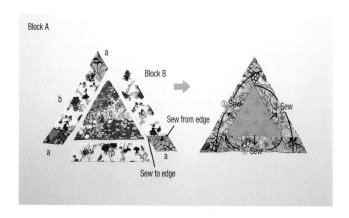

2 Sew together two of the blocks from step 1 working from edge to edge, creating a parallelogram. Make four blocks.

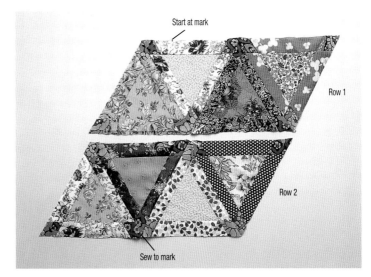

3 Sew two blocks from step 2 side by side. Make two blocks.

4 Sew together the two Row Blocks from mark to mark. A star appears at the center of the pieces sewn together. Let the seam allowances fall into the shape of a pinwheel. The pattern is complete.

Tools

Thick white yarn

Trapunto tweezers (or hemostat)

Trapunto needle

Trapunto is a technique that creates three-dimensional effects in fabric by filling sections of stitching with material such as yarn. To better illustrate the technique, red yarn is used in the photos.

Plan the Trapunto

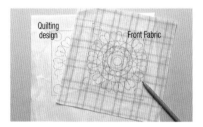

Quilting design

Front Fabric

1 Copy the quilting design onto the front fabric using a water-soluble marking pen.

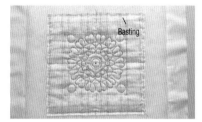

Basting

2 Layer the the back fabric, the batting, and the front fabric from step 1, then baste together. Stitch the quilting, and when finished, remove the basting.

3 Wash the quilt to remove the marking pen. Let dry (not in direct sunlight). See page 75 for washing instructions.

Create the Trapunto

From the back side of the quilt, pass double-threaded yarn between the back fabric and the batting.

Fill the center circle:

1 Insert the needle on one side of the center circle of the design and pull it through from the opposite side.

2 Tug the yarn to pull it to the center, then trim it flush with the circle's edge.

3 Using the tweezers (or hemostat), tuck the yarn in on both edges.

4 Make two parallel passes with the yarn below the first strand.

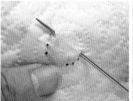

5 Repeat step 4 above the first strand of yarn.

Fill the second ring:

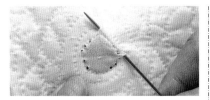

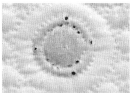

Yarn end

1 The perimeter of the circle will be filled in four sections. First, pass the yarn through about ¼ of the outer circle. When trimming yarn, keep a bit of the end sticking out.

2 Insert the needle in the same exit hole from step 1, and fill about ¼ of the circle. Repeat until the circle is full. Finish by drawing the needle out at the same place you began. Cut the yarn at the edge of the fabric. Using the tweezers (or hemostat), stuff all yarn ends to the inside.

Fill the third ring:

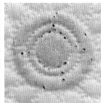

This ring is wider, so it is filled in two rounds. As illustrated for the second ring, divide the circle into four sections and pass the yarn through. To the outside of this, pass the yarn through once more in the same way.

Fill the fourth ring (small circles):

Fill the small circles that comprise the fourth ring of the design. Pass the yarn once through the center of each circle, then once above and below the yarn.

Fill the triangles:

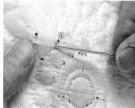
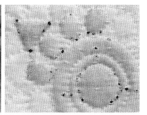

See the diagram (above). Pass the yarn through from ① and then ②, then cut at the edge. For ③, insert the needle at the same point as ① and pull it through at the tip of the triangle (on the side of ②), then cut the yarn. For ④, pass the yarn through at an angle, filling in the gap.

Fill the hearts:

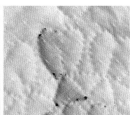
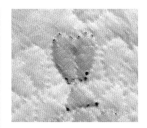

Wrong Side

1 From the center of the left side, pass the yarn vertically three times.

2 On the right side, pass the yarn vertically three times again.

3 The outermost circles are filled in the same way as the center circle. The trapunto is now complete.

Instructions for the Quilts

Scrap Star

Quilt on page 35
Finished Dimensions 17¹¹/₁₆" × 17¹¹/₁₆" (44.9 × 44.9 cm)
Patterns (see insert): side A

Materials

COTTON FABRIC

Five different print fabrics (pattern)	as needed
Green print (Piece a and b)	43⁵/₁₆" × 7⅞" (110 × 20 cm)
Checkered print (Piece a and b, binding fabric)	43⁵/₁₆" × 7⅞" (110 × 20 cm)
Print (back fabric)	21⅝" × 21⅝" (55 × 55 cm)

BATTING

Batting	21⅝" × 21⅝" (55 × 55 cm)

Cutting measurements for borders and binding are on the Quilt Diagrams.

Instructions

1. Using the five prints, make four scrap star patterns (see page 82).

2. Using the green print and checkered fabric, make nine of the nine-patch square pattern.

3. Using the same fabric as step 2, make 12 of pattern A.

4. Make three rows of a block consisting of five pieces of the nine-patch pattern alternating with pattern A, joined side by side. (Row 1, Row 2, and Row 3).

5. Alternate pattern A and the scrap star pattern and join the five pieces side by side to make 2 rows. (Row 2 and Row 4).

6. Sew together the five rows and finish the top. (See assembly diagram.)

7. Draw the quilting lines, then layer the back fabric, the batting, and the top fabric from step 6. Baste, then quilt. Trim the extra batting and back fabric to align with the quilt top.

8. Prepare the checkered fabric 1⅜" (3.5 cm) in width and 70⅞" (180 cm) in length (for the binding). Finish quilt by wrapping the perimeter of the quilt with the binding. (See page 74).

Quilt Diagram: Rows

Nine Patch   Scrap Star   Pattern A

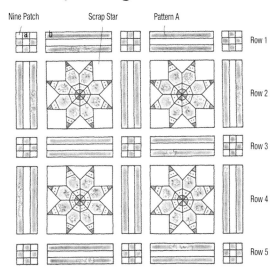

Row 1

Row 2

Row 3

Row 4

Row 5

Quilt Diagram

¼"
(6 mm)

Binding
(checkered fabric)

(green print)

(checkered fabric)

Use rocking stitch for each piece

17⅛"
(43.5 cm)

6" (15 cm)

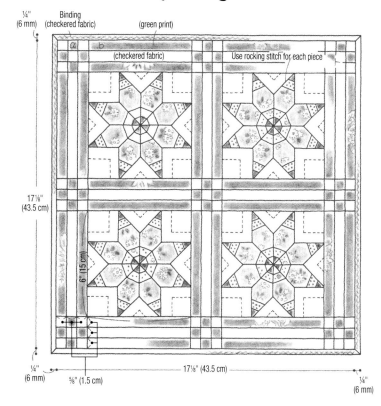

¼"
(6 mm)

⅝" (1.5 cm)

17⅛" (43.5 cm)

¼"
(6 mm)

One of each: Front Fabric (Patchwork), Quilting Lines, Back Fabric (Print)

Cut pieces with a ¼" (6 mm) seam allowance.

Prepare 21⅝" × 21⅝" (55 x 55 cm) of the back fabric and batting.

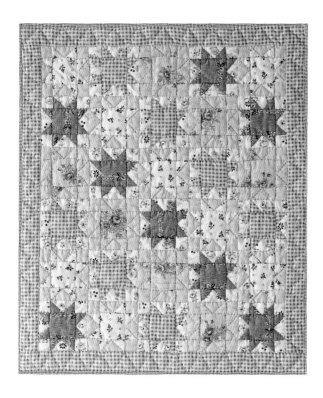

Lone Star

Quilt on page 51
Finished Dimensions 19$\frac{1}{16}$" × 16$\frac{5}{16}$" (48.4 × 41.4 cm)
Full-size template: page 85

Materials

COTTON FABRIC

Checkered a (pattern, border)	43$\frac{5}{16}$" × 11$\frac{13}{16}$" (110 × 30 cm)
Print a·b·c·d (pattern), Pink (no print)	as needed
Checkered b (binding fabric)	2$\frac{3}{4}$" × 43$\frac{5}{16}$" (7 × 110 cm)
Print (back fabric)	21$\frac{5}{8}$" × 19$\frac{11}{16}$" (55 × 50 cm)

BATTING

Batting	21$\frac{5}{8}$" × 19$\frac{11}{16}$" (55 × 50 cm)

Cutting measurements for borders and binding are on the Quilt Diagrams.

Instructions

1. Using each of the prints and checkered a, make 30 Lone Star patterns (see page 84).

2. Make six rows, each with five Lone Star patterns sewn side by side.

3. Sew together the six rows to make the center block. (See the quilt assembly diagram for the color arrangement.)

4. In order: sew Border A to the left and right of the center block, and Border B to the top and bottom. Finish the top piece.

5. Draw the quilting lines. Layer the back fabric, batting, and top piece. Baste, then quilt. Use a rocking stitch to quilt along each piece; within the borders, quilt a zig-zag pattern (see the diagram).

6. Trim the extra back fabric and batting to the edges of the top piece. Wrap the perimeter with the 1$\frac{3}{8}$" (3.5 cm) -wide binding fabric to finish.

Quilt Diagram

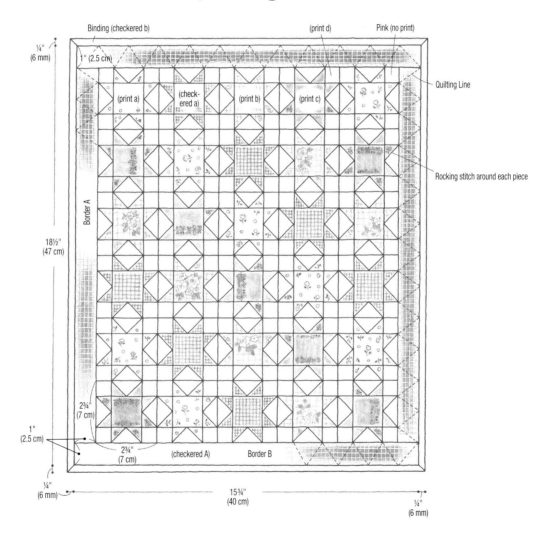

Binding (checkered b)　　(print d)　　Pink (no print)

¼" (6 mm)

1" (2.5 cm)

(print a)　(checkered a)　(print b)　(print c)

Quilting Line

Rocking stitch around each piece

Border A

18½" (47 cm)

2¾" (7 cm)

1" (2.5 cm)

2¾" (7 cm)　　(checkered A)　　Border B

¼" (6 mm)

15¾" (40 cm)

¼" (6 mm)

¼" (6 mm)

One of each: Front Fabric (Patchwork), Batting, Back Fabric (Print)

Cut pieces with a ¼" (6 mm) seam allowance.

Prepare 21⅝" × 19¹¹⁄₁₆" (55 × 50 cm) of the back fabric and batting.

Mini-Quilts

Star Blossom

Quilt on page 34
Finished Dimensions 22³⁄₁₆" × 16⁵⁄₁₆" (56.4 × 41.4 cm)
Full-size pattern: side A (see insert)

Materials

COTTON FABRIC

Four different print fabrics (pattern)	as needed
Print (border)	43⁵⁄₁₆" × 5⁷⁄₈" (110 × 15 cm)
Checkered print (binding fabric)	3⁵⁄₁₆" × 43⁵⁄₁₆" (10 × 110 cm)
Print (back fabric)	23⁵⁄₈" × 19¹¹⁄₁₆" (60 × 50 cm)

BATTING

Batting	23⁵⁄₈" × 19¹¹⁄₁₆" (60 × 50 cm)

Cutting measurements for borders and binding are on the Quilt Diagrams.

Instructions

1. Make six Star Blossom Patterns (see page 86). Sew together to create the center block (see assembly diagram).

2. Align and sew Border A to the left and right of the block from step 1, and Border B to the top and bottom, finishing the top piece. (See Quilt Diagram.)

3. Draw the quilting lines and layer the back fabric, batting, and quilt top piece. Baste, then quilt each piece using a rocking stitch. Quilt around the border.

4. Trim the extra back fabric and batting to the edges of the top piece. Wrap the perimeter with the 1³⁄₈" (3.5 cm) -wide binding fabric to finish.

Sewing the Border

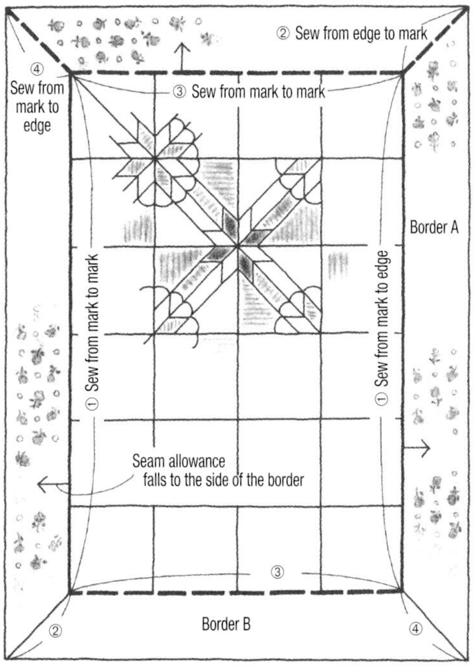
④
Sew from mark to edge
② Sew from edge to mark
③ Sew from mark to mark
Border A
① Sew from mark to mark
① Sew from mark to edge
Seam allowance falls to the side of the border
③
②
Border B
④

Quilt Diagram

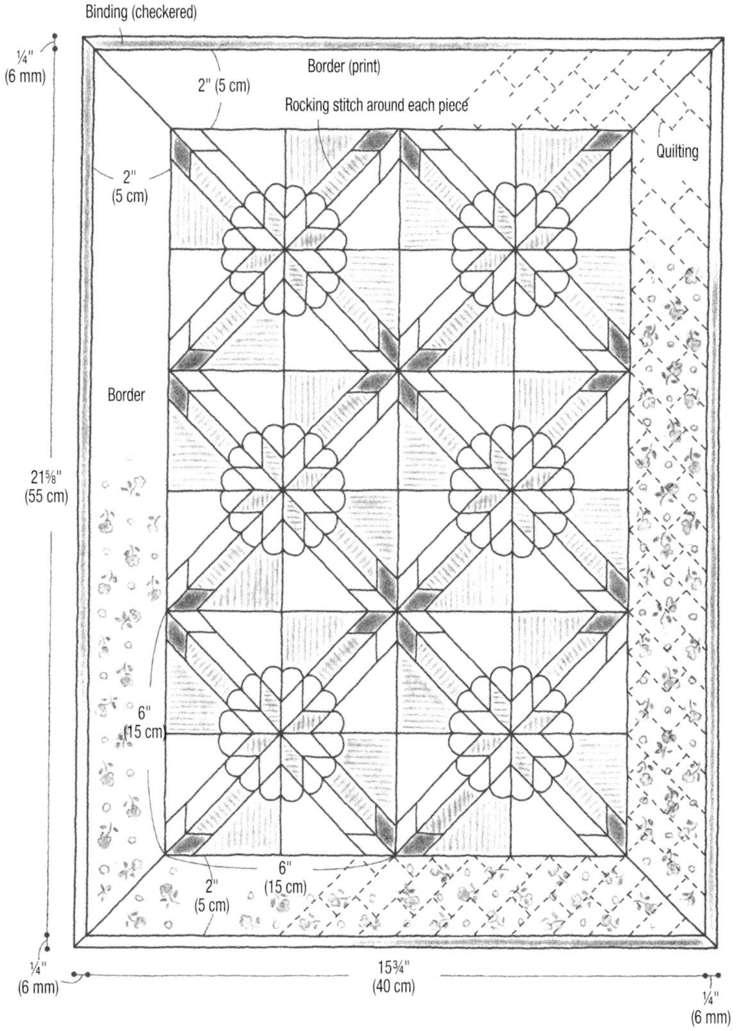
Binding (checkered)
¼" (6 mm)
Border (print)
2" (5 cm)
Rocking stitch around each piece
Quilting
2" (5 cm)
Border
21⅝" (55 cm)
6" (15 cm)
6" (15 cm)
2" (5 cm)
¼" (6 mm)
15¾" (40 cm)
¼" (6 mm)

One of each: Front Fabric (Patchwork), Quilt Fabric, Back Fabric (Print)

Cut pieces with a ¼" (6 mm) seam allowance.

Prepare 23⅝" × 19¹¹⁄₁₆" (60 × 50 cm) of the back fabric and batting.

Stardust Memory

Quilt on page 51
Finished Dimensions 20¼" × 16⁵⁄₁₆" (51.4 × 41.4 cm)
Full-size pattern: side A (see insert)

Materials

COTTON FABRIC

Five different print fabrics (pieces)	as needed
Print (piece, border)	43⁵⁄₁₆" × 5⅞" (110 × 15 cm)
Print (binding)	2¾" × 43⁵⁄₁₆" (7 × 110 cm)
Print (back fabric)	21⅝" × 17¾" (55 × 45 cm)

BATTING

Batting	21⅝" × 17¾" (55 × 45 cm)

Cutting measurements for borders and binding are on the Quilt Diagrams.

Instructions

1. Make 12 of the Stardust Memory Pattern (see page 88), six of Pattern B, four of Pattern B①, and ten of Pattern B②.

2. Sew together A·B·B①·B② patterns diagonally to create eight rows (see the diagram).

3. Using an outline satin stitch, sew together the eight rows to form the center block.

4. Cut out Borders A and B from the print. In order: sew Border A to the left and right of the center block, and Border B to the top and bottom, using an outline satin stitch. The seam allowance should fall to the side of the borders. The top piece is complete.

5. Draw the quilting lines and layer the back fabric, batting, and quilt top piece. Baste, and quilt each piece using a rocking stitch. Within the border, quilt a lattice shape.

6. Trim the extra back fabric and batting to the edges of the quilt top. Wrap the perimeter with the 1⅜" (3.5 cm) -wide binding to finish.

Sew the Center Block

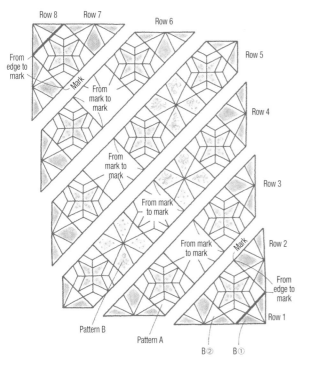

Row 8   Row 7

Row 6

Row 5

From edge to mark

Mark

From mark to mark

Row 4

From mark to mark

Row 3

From mark to mark

From mark to mark

Mark

Row 2

From edge to mark

Pattern B

Pattern A

B②   B①

Row 1

Quilt Diagram

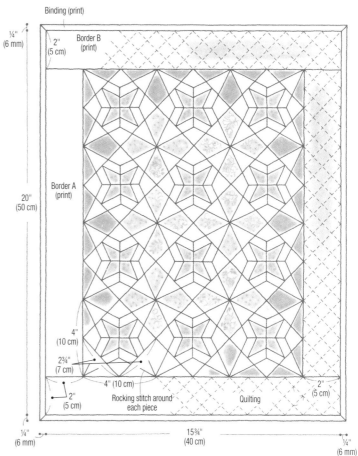

Binding (print)

¼"
(6 mm)

2"
(5 cm)

Border B
(print)

Border A
(print)

20"
(50 cm)

4"
(10 cm)

2¾"
(7 cm)

4" (10 cm)

2"
(5 cm)

Rocking stitch around
each piece

Quilting

2"
(5 cm)

¼"
(6 mm)

15¾"
(40 cm)

¼"
(6 mm)

One of each: Front Fabric (Patchwork), Batting, Back Fabric (Print)

Cut pieces with a ¼" (6 mm) seam allowance.

Prepare 21⅝" × 17¾" (55 × 45 cm) of the back fabric and batting.

Wandering Diamond

Quilt on page 44
Finished Dimensions 20⅝" × 16⁵⁄₁₆" (52.4 × 41.4 cm)
Full-size pattern: side A (see insert)

Materials

COTTON FABRIC

Four different print fabrics (pieces)	as needed
Flower print (square pieces)	7¹⁄₁₆" × 21¼" (18 × 54 cm)
Blue print (border, binding fabric)	43⁵⁄₁₆" × 4¾" (110 × 12 cm)
Print (back fabric)	23⅝" × 19¹¹⁄₁₆" (60 × 50 cm)

BATTING

Batting	23⅝" × 19¹¹⁄₁₆" (60 × 50 cm)

Cutting measurements for borders and binding are on the Quilt Diagrams.

Instructions

1. Make six of the Wandering Diamond Pattern (see page 90), however, do not sew the outermost diamond shapes. Cut out 12 of the square pieces.

2. Arrange the patterns from step 1, joined at the diamonds, and sew together with the square pieces.

3. Make ten of the Wandering Diamond Pattern A, and four of Pattern B, and then sew together in the same way to the block from step 2.

4. Sew on the border to the block from step 3. (See the diagram on page 70 for instructions on sewing the border.) The quilt top is complete.

5. Draw the quilting lines and layer the back fabric, batting, and quilt top piece. Baste, and quilt.

6. Trim the extra back fabric and batting to the edges of the quilt top. Wrap the perimeter with the 1⅜" (3.5 cm) -wide binding to finish.

Quilt Diagram

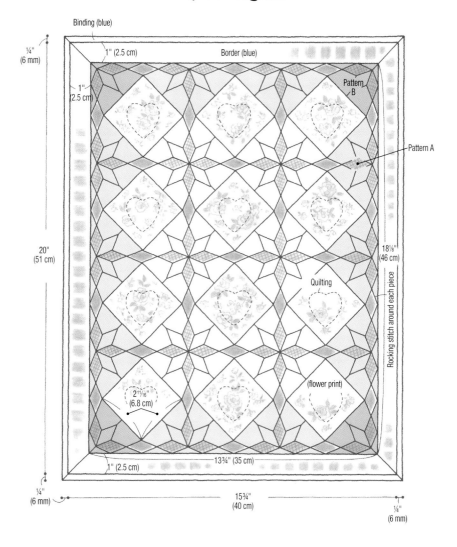

Binding (blue)

¼" (6 mm)

1" (2.5 cm)

Border (blue)

1" (2.5 cm)

Pattern B

Pattern A

20" (51 cm)

18⅛" (46 cm)

Rocking stitch around each piece

Quilting

(flower print)

2¹¹⁄₁₆" (6.8 cm)

1" (2.5 cm)

13¾" (35 cm)

¼" (6 mm)

15¾" (40 cm)

¼" (6 mm)

One of each: Front Fabric (Patchwork), Batting, Back Fabric (Print)

Cut pieces with a ¼" (6 mm) seam allowance.

Prepare 23⅝" × 19¹¹⁄₁₆" (60 × 50 cm) of the back fabric and batting.

Mini-Quilts

Shooting Star I

Quilt on page 53
Finished Dimensions 20⅝" × 16⅝⁶" (52.4 × 41.4 cm)
Full-size pattern: side A (see insert)

Materials

COTTON FABRIC

Print (several styles)	as needed (pieces a·c)
Flower print (pieces b·c·d·e, border A·B)	43⁵⁄₁₆" × 11¹³⁄₁₆" (110 × 30 cm)
Purple print (lattice)	3⁵⁄₁₆" × 43⁵⁄₁₆" (10 × 110 cm)
Paisley print (lattice, border)	7⅞" × 19¹¹⁄₁₆" (20 × 55 cm)
Dot print (binding fabric)	2¾" × 43⁵⁄₁₆" (7 × 110 cm)
Print (back fabric)	23⅝" × 19¹¹⁄₁₆" (60 × 50 cm)

BATTING

Batting	23⅝" × 19¹¹⁄₁₆" (60 × 50 cm)

Cutting measurements for borders and binding are on the Quilt Diagrams.

Instructions

1. Make 18 of the Shooting Star Pattern I (see insert side A).

2. Make the center block by diagonally arranging and sewing pieces d·e and the pattern from step 1, and laying strips of lattice in between. (See page 112 for instructions for sewing the block.)

3. Fit within the border and sew together to finish the quilt top piece.

4. Draw the quilting lines. Layer the back fabric, batting, and quilt top piece. Baste, then quilt.

5. Trim the extra back fabric and batting to the edges of the top piece. Wrap the perimeter with the 1⅜" (3.5 cm) -wide binding to finish.

Quilt Diagram

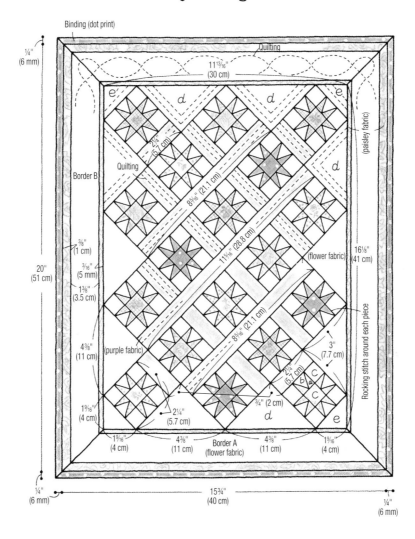

Binding (dot print)

Quilting

11¹³⁄₁₆"
(30 cm)

¼"
(6 mm)

e · d · d · e

2¼
(5.7 cm)

(paisley fabric)

Border B

Quilting

8⁵⁄₁₆" (21.1 cm)

d

11⁵⁄₁₆" (28.8 cm)

16⅛"
(41 cm)

⅜"
(1 cm)

³⁄₁₆"
(5 mm)

1⅜"
(3.5 cm)

(flower fabric)

20"
(51 cm)

8⁵⁄₁₆" (21.1 cm)

Rocking stitch around each piece

4⅜"
(11 cm)

(purple fabric)

3"
(7.7 cm)

2¼
(5.7 cm)

C

b a

C

1⁹⁄₁₆"
(4 cm)

2¼"
(5.7 cm)

¾" (2 cm)

d

e

1⁹⁄₁₆"
(4 cm)

4⅜"
(11 cm)

Border A
(flower fabric)

4⅜"
(11 cm)

1⁹⁄₁₆"
(4 cm)

¼"
(6 mm)

15¾"
(40 cm)

¼"
(6 mm)

One of each: Front Fabric (Patchwork), Batting, Back Fabric (Print)

Cut pieces with a ¼" (6 mm) seam allowance.

Prepare 23⅝" × 19¹¹⁄₁₆" (60 × 50 cm) of the back fabric and batting.

Milky Way and Log Cabin

Quilt on page 32
Finished Dimensions 21¹³⁄₁₆" × 16½" (55.4 × 41.9 cm)
Full-size pattern: side A (see insert)

Materials

COTTON FABRIC

Six different prints (pieces)	as needed
Checkered (binding fabric)	2¾" × 43⁵⁄₁₆" (7 × 110 cm)
Print (back fabric)	23⅝" × 17¾" (60 × 45 cm)

BATTING

Batting	23⅝" × 17¾" (60 × 45 cm)

Cutting measurements for borders and binding are on the Quilt Diagrams.

Instructions

1. Make 12 of the Milky Way and Log Cabin Pattern (see page 94).

2. Per the Quilt Diagram, sew together the 12 patterns to make the quilt top piece.

3. Layer the back fabric, batting, and quilt top piece into three layers and baste. Using a rocking stitch, quilt around each piece.

4. Remove the basting, then trim any extra back fabric and batting to the edges of the top piece.

5. Prepare 2.2 yd (2 m) of the 1⅜" (3.5 cm) -wide checkered binding fabric. Wrap it around the perimeter and finish.

Quilt Diagram

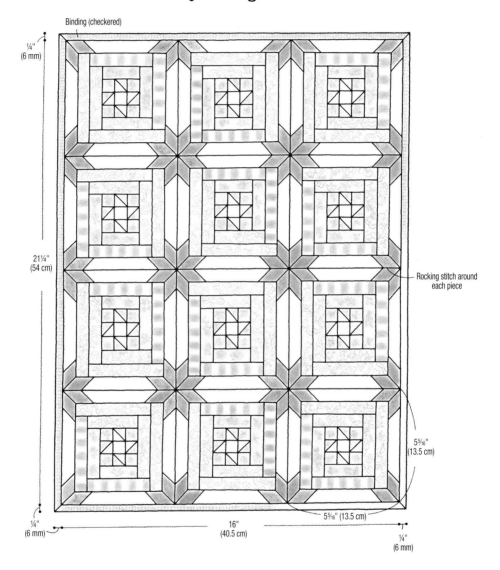

One of each: Front Fabric (Patchwork), Batting, Back Fabric (Print)

Cut pieces with a ¼" (6 mm) seam allowance.

Prepare 23⅝" × 17¾" (60 × 45 cm) of the back fabric and batting.

Martha Washington Star

Quilt on page 32
Finished Dimensions 24⅜" × 16⅝" (62 × 42.2 cm)
Full-size pattern: side A (see insert and facing page)

Materials

COTTON FABRIC

Checkered (several styles, pieces)	as needed
Dark red print (Piece a, border, binding fabric)	43⁵⁄₁₆" × 7⅞" (110 × 20 cm)
Brown print (lattice)	43⁵⁄₁₆" × 5⅞" (110 × 15 cm)
Print (back fabric)	25⅝" × 17¾" (65 × 45 cm)

BATTING

Batting	25⅝" × 17¾" (65 × 45 cm)

Cutting measurements for borders and binding are on the Quilt Diagrams.

Instructions

1. Make six of the Martha Washington Star Patterns (Pattern ①; see page 96). Pattern ② is made by sewing together four a Pieces. Make six of Pattern ② to be used with Lattice a, then change color patterns and make 34 of Pattern ② for use as Lattice c.

2. Alternate Lattice a and Pattern ①, and sew the five pieces together side by side to form three rows (Row 1, Row 3, and Row 5). Next, alternate Pattern ② and Lattice a, and sew together to form two blocks (Row 2 and Row 4).

3. Sew together Rows 1–5 to form the center block. Sew Border A to the left and right side.

4. Sew together side by side 17 of the Pattern a. Make two of these Lattice c.

5. Sew together Lattices b–c and Border B, making the two top and bottom blocks. Sew these blocks to the top and bottom of the center block, finishing the quilt top piece.

6. Layer the back fabric, batting, and quilt top piece. Baste, then using a rocking stitch, quilt around each piece. Trim the extra back fabric and batting to the edges of the top piece. Wrap the perimeter with the 1⅜" (3.5 cm) -wide binding fabric to finish.

Quilt Diagram

Binding (dark red print)

¼" (6 mm)

1" (2.4 cm) Border B (dark red print)

⅝" (1.5 cm)

Lattice b   Lattice c

Lattice a

(brown print)

Border A (dark red print)

Pattern ①

Piece a

18⅞" (48 cm)

23⅞" (60.6 cm)

Rocking stitch around each piece

1" (2.4 cm)

5¹¹⁄₁₆" (14.4 cm)

1" (2.4 cm)

1" (2.4 cm)
⅝" (1.5 cm)
1" (2.4 cm)

1" (2.4 cm)

1" (2.4 cm)

¼" (6 mm)

5¹¹⁄₁₆" (14.4 cm)

16" (40.8 cm)

¼" (6 mm)

Sewing Guide (Quilt Top)

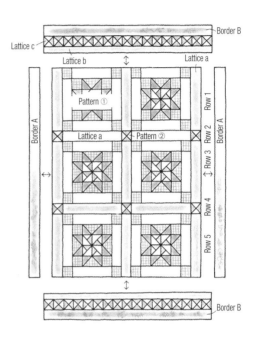

Border B

Lattice c

Lattice b   Lattice a

Pattern ①

Border A

Lattice a   Pattern ②

Border A

Row 1
Row 2
Row 3
Row 4
Row 5

Border B

One of each: Front Fabric (Patchwork), Batting, Back Fabric (Print)

Cut pieces with a ¼" (6 mm) seam allowance.

Prepare 25⅝" × 17¾" (65 × 45 cm) of the back fabric and batting.

Paper Pattern Guide ②

a

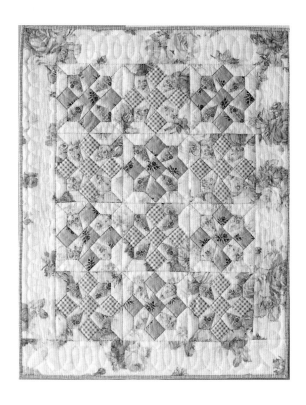

Mini-Quilts

Shooting Star II

Quilt on page 53
Finished Dimensions 20¼" × 16¹⁵⁄₁₆" (51.4 × 41.4 cm)
Full-size pattern: side A (see insert)

Materials

COTTON FABRIC

Six different prints (pieces)	as needed
Flower print (border)	43⁵⁄₁₆" × 3⁵⁄₁₆" (110 × 10 cm)
Checkered (binding fabric)	2¾" × 43⁵⁄₁₆" (7 × 110 cm)
Print (back fabric)	23⅝" × 19¹¹⁄₁₆" (60 × 50 cm)

BATTING

Batting	23⅝" × 19¹¹⁄₁₆" (60 × 50 cm)

Cutting measurements for borders and binding are on the Quilt Diagrams.

Instructions

1. Using two different color schemes, make six each of the Shooting Star Pattern (see page 92).

2. Referring to the Quilt Diagram, arrange the 12 patterns to form the center block.

3. In order: sew Border A to the left and right side, and then Border B to the top and bottom of the center block. The top piece is complete.

4. Draw the quilting lines and layer the back fabric, batting, and quilt top piece. Baste, then quilt.

5. Trim the extra back fabric and batting to the edges of the top piece. Wrap the perimeter with the 1⅜" (3.5 cm) -wide binding fabric to finish.

Quilt Diagram

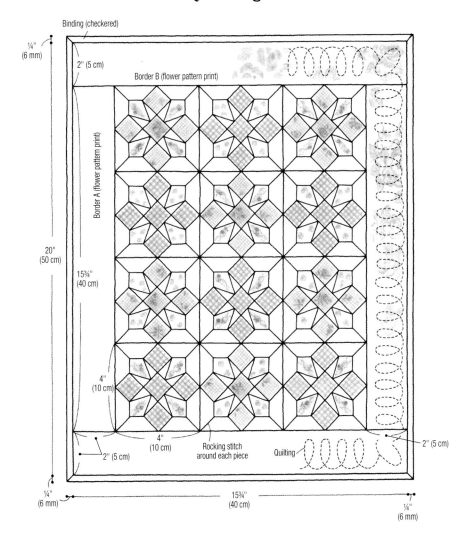

Binding (checkered)

¼"
(6 mm)

2" (5 cm)

Border B (flower pattern print)

Border A (flower pattern print)

20"
(50 cm)

15¾"
(40 cm)

4"
(10 cm)

4"
(10 cm)

Rocking stitch
around each piece

Quilting

2" (5 cm)

2" (5 cm)

¼"
(6 mm)

15¾"
(40 cm)

¼"
(6 mm)

One of each: Front Fabric (Patchwork), Batting, Back Fabric (Print)

Cut pieces with a ¼" (6 mm) seam allowance.

Prepare 23⅝" × 19¹¹⁄₁₆" (60 × 50 cm) of the back fabric and batting.

Broken Star

Quilt on page 54
Finished Dimensions 18¼" × 18¼" (46.4 × 46.4 cm)
Full-size pattern: side A (see insert)

Materials

COTTON FABRIC

Light purple with small flowers (pieces, border)	43⁵⁄₁₆" × 7⅞" (110 × 20 cm)
Purple with small flowers (pieces, border, binding fabric)	43⁵⁄₁₆" × 15 ¾" (110 × 40 cm)
White with small blue flowers (pieces)	43⁵⁄₁₆" × 7⅞" (110 × 20 cm)
Dot print (pieces)	43⁵⁄₁₆" × 3⁵⁄₁₆" (110 × 10 cm)
White with small pink flowers (pieces)	7⅞" × 21⅝" (20 × 55 cm)
Print (back fabric)	21⅝" × 21⅝" (55 × 55 cm)

BATTING

Batting	21⅝" × 21⅝" (55 × 55 cm)

Cutting measurements for borders and binding are on the Quilt Diagrams.

Instructions

1. Sew the Eight-Point Star for the center (①). Then sew Patterns ② – ⑪ to form the center block.

2. Make the borders. First, make the four-path pattern for the four corners. Next, sew together Border Pieces a–b and make four of Block A.

3. Take two of Block As from step 2 and sew a four-patch pattern to the left and right sides. Make two of Block B.

4. Using an outline satin stitch, sew the two Block As from step 2 to the right and left sides of the center block from step 1. Next, sew the two Block Bs from step 3 to the top and bottom using an outline satin stitch. The quilt top piece is finished.

5. Draw the quilting line. Layer the back fabric, batting, and quilt top piece. Baste, then quilt.

6. Trim the extra back fabric and batting to the edges of the top piece. Wrap the perimeter with the 1⅜" (3.5 cm) -wide binding fabric to finish.

Quilt Diagram

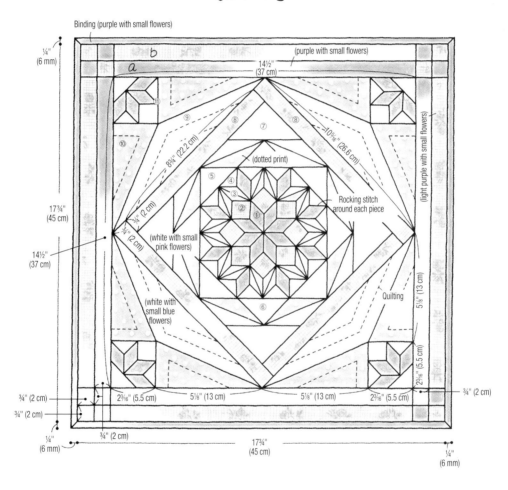

Binding (purple with small flowers)

¼" (6 mm)

(purple with small flowers)

b

a

14½" (37 cm)

⑪

⑨

⑧

⑦

⑧

10⅝" (26.6 cm)

(light purple with small flowers)

⑩

8¾" (22.2 cm)

(dotted print)

⑤

④

③

②

①

Rocking stitch around each piece

17¾" (45 cm)

¾" (2 cm)

¾" (2 cm)

(white with small pink flowers)

14½" (37 cm)

(white with small blue flowers)

⑥

Quilting

5⅛" (13 cm)

2³⁄₁₆" (5.5 cm)

¾" (2 cm)

¾" (2 cm)

2³⁄₁₆" (5.5 cm)

5⅛" (13 cm)

5⅛" (13 cm)

2³⁄₁₆" (5.5 cm)

¾" (2 cm)

¼" (6 mm)

¾" (2 cm)

17¾" (45 cm)

¼" (6 mm)

One of each: Front Fabric (Patchwork), Batting, Back Fabric (Print)

Cut pieces with a ¼" (6 mm) seam allowance.

Prepare 21⅝" × 21⅝" (55 × 55 cm) of the back fabric and batting.

Spring Star

Quilt on page 53
Finished Dimensions 18¼" × 18¼" (46.4 × 46.4 cm)
Full-size pattern: side A (see insert)

Materials

COTTON FABRIC

Various prints (tulip pattern, Piece a)	as needed
Flower print (border)	11¹³⁄₁₆" × 19¹¹⁄₁₆" (30 × 50 cm)
Striped (border)	5⅞" × 19¹¹⁄₁₆" (15 × 50 cm)
Print (binding)	2¾" × 43⁵⁄₁₆" (7 × 110 cm)
Print (back fabric)	21⅝" × 21⅝" (55 × 55 cm)

BATTING

Batting	21⅝" × 21⅝" (55 × 55 cm)

Cutting measurements for borders and binding are on the Quilt Diagrams.

Instructions

1. Make eight of the Tulip Pattern (see page 98).

2. Sew together the diamond shapes to make a Bethlehem Star, and then fit it together with the pattern from step 1.

3. Fit in the borders and sew together around the block from step 2, finishing the quilt top piece.

4. Layer the back fabric, batting, and quilt top piece. Baste, then quilt around the pieces using a rocking stitch.

5. Trim the extra back fabric and batting to the edges of the top piece. Wrap the perimeter with the 1⅜" (3.5 cm) -wide binding fabric to finish.

Quilt Diagram

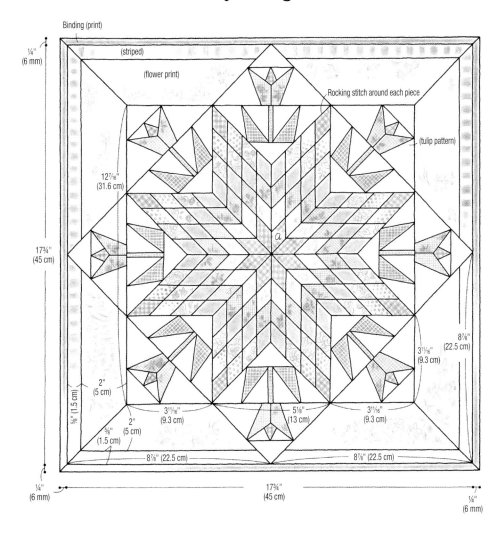

Binding (print)

¼" (6 mm)

(striped)

(flower print)

Rocking stitch around each piece

(tulip pattern)

12⁷⁄₁₆" (31.6 cm)

17¾" (45 cm)

8⁷⁄₈" (22.5 cm)

3¹¹⁄₁₆" (9.3 cm)

5⁄₈" (1.5 cm)

2" (5 cm)

2" (5 cm)

5⁄₈" (1.5 cm)

3¹¹⁄₁₆" (9.3 cm)

5⅛" (13 cm)

3¹¹⁄₁₆" (9.3 cm)

8⁷⁄₈" (22.5 cm)

8⁷⁄₈" (22.5 cm)

¼" (6 mm)

17¾" (45 cm)

¼" (6 mm)

One of each: Front Fabric (Patchwork), Batting, Back Fabric (Print)

Cut pieces with a ¼" (6 mm) seam allowance.

Prepare 21⅝" × 21⅝" (55 × 55 cm) of the back fabric and batting.

Star Flower Basket

Quilt on page 33

Finished Dimensions 21" × 17¹⁄₁₆" (53.4 × 43.4 cm)

Pattern: side A (see insert and facing page)

Materials

COTTON FABRIC

White with small white flowers (appliqué base, pieces)	43⁵⁄₁₆" × 9⅞" (110 × 25 cm)
Dotted print (pieces)	43⁵⁄₁₆" × 9⅞" (110 × 25 cm)
Print a (pieces)	43⁵⁄₁₆" × 7⅞" (110 × 20 cm)
Print b·c, green print (pieces, appliqué fabric)	as needed
Print d (binding)	2¾" × 43⁵⁄₁₆" (7 × 110 cm)
Print (back fabric)	25⅝" × 21⅝" (65 × 55 cm)

BATTING

Batting	22" × 21⅝" (56 × 55 cm)

Cutting measurements for borders and binding are on the Quilt Diagrams.

Instructions

1. Doing piecework, make the base for the appliqué for A.

2. On the appliqué for B, create the stem, leaves, and buds.

3. Sew together the appliqué bases for c·d. Then sew together the appliqué base from step 2.

4. Make the flower pattern, then sew together with the base from step 3.

5. Sew together the bases from step 4 and step 1. The center block is complete.

6. Doing piecework, make the border. Sew the border around the center block from left to right, top and bottom. The top piece is finished.

7. Draw the quilting lines. Layer the back fabric, batting, and quilt top piece. Baste, then quilt.

8. Trim the extra back fabric and batting to the edges of the top piece. Wrap the perimeter with the 1⅜" (3.5 cm) -wide binding fabric to finish.

Quilt Diagram

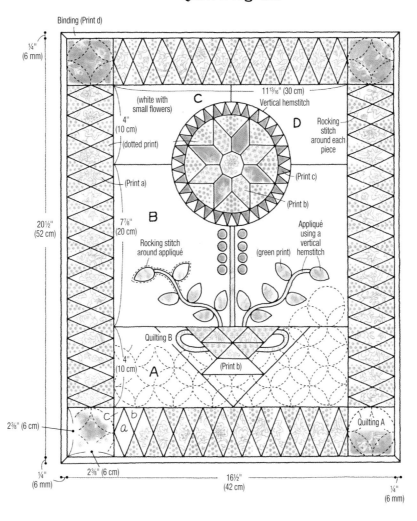

Binding (Print d)

¼" (6 mm)

11¹³⁄₁₆" (30 cm)
Vertical hemstitch

C

D

Rocking stitch around each piece

(white with small flowers)

4" (10 cm)

(dotted print)

(Print a)

(Print c)

(Print b)

20½" (52 cm)

7⅞" (20 cm)

B

Rocking stitch around appliqué

Appliqué using a vertical hemstitch

(green print)

Quilting B

4" (10 cm)

A

(Print b)

c b
a

2⅜" (6 cm)

Quilting A

¼" (6 mm)

2⅜" (6 cm)

16½" (42 cm)

¼" (6 mm)

One of each: Front Fabric (Patchwork, Appliqué), Batting, Back Fabric (Print)

Cut pieces with a ¼" (6 mm) seam allowance and the appliqué with a ⅛" (3 mm) allowance.

Prepare 25⅝" × 21⅝" (65 × 55 cm) of the back fabric and batting.

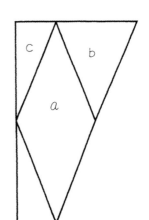

Paper Pattern Guide for the Border

Cut pieces with a ¼" (6 mm) seam allowance.

Mini-Quilts

Feathered Star Tree

Quilt on page 55
Finished Dimensions 18¼" × 18¼" (46.4 × 46.4 cm)
Pattern: side A (see insert)

Materials

COTTON FABRIC

Dotted print (pieces, border)	43⁵⁄₁₆" × 5⅞" (110 × 15 cm)
Various prints (pieces, border)	as needed
Print (binding)	2¾" × 43⁵⁄₁₆" (7 × 110 cm)
Print (back fabric)	21⅝" × 21⅝" (55 × 55 cm)

BATTING

Batting	21⅝" × 21⅝" (55 × 55 cm)

Cutting measurements for borders and binding are on the Quilt Diagrams.

Instructions

1. Make the center pattern. Sew together eight pieces to form the Star Pattern (①). Fit in the triangular pieces and sew together (②).

2. Sew the Tree Trunk Block to the block from step 1, and then sew the large triangular pieces around that (③).

3. Sew the squares that go between the trees (④).

4. Make 16 blocks of the small triangles sewn together. Sew those around the large triangles (⑤).

5. Fit in and sew the square pieces around the block from step 4 (⑥). The center block is now complete.

6. Following Steps 1–4, make the top left, bottom left, top right, and bottom right patterns, each missing one quarter of the design. Fit these pieces to the block from step 5 and sew together.

7. Insert the square and triangular blocks around the pattern from step 6 to make the center block. Sew on the border. The quilt top piece is finished.

8. Draw the quilting lines. Layer the back fabric, batting, and quilt top piece. Baste, then quilt.

9. Trim the extra back fabric and batting to the edges of the top piece. Wrap the perimeter with the 1⅜" (3.5 cm) -wide binding fabric to finish.

Sewing Guide

Quilt Diagram

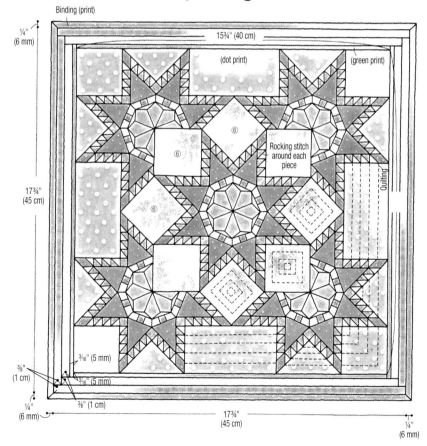

One of each: Front Fabric (Patchwork), Batting, Back Fabric (Print)

Cut pieces with a ¼" (6 mm) seam allowance.

Prepare 21⅝" × 21⅝" (55 × 55 cm) of the back fabric and batting.

Pinwheel Star

Quilt on page 50
Finished Dimensions 18¼" × 18¼" (46.4 × 46.4 cm)
Full-size pattern: side A (see insert and facing page)

Materials

COTTON FABRIC

Striped (border)	43⁵⁄₁₆" × 5⅞" (110 × 15 cm)
Flower print (pieces)	43⁵⁄₁₆" × 7⅞" (110 × 20 cm)
Purple with small flowers (pieces)	43⁵⁄₁₆" × 3⁵⁄₁₆" (110 × 10 cm)
Various prints (pieces)	as needed
Checkered print (binding fabric)	2¾" × 43⁵⁄₁₆" (7 × 110 cm)
Print (back fabric)	21⅝" × 21⅝" (55 × 55 cm)

BATTING

Batting	21⅝" × 21⅝" (55 × 55 cm)

Cutting measurements for borders and binding are on the Quilt Diagrams.

Instructions

1. Make the Pinwheel Star Pattern (see page 100). Around the pattern sew the triangular c Pieces, creating a larger square that measures 8½" (21.5 cm) along the sides.

2. Make four Daisy Patterns.

3. Appliqué the Daisy Patterns to Piece d. Be sure to cut the Daisy Pattern and Piece d with a ¼" (6 mm) seam allowance. Make four of these patterns.

4. Sew on the patterns from step 3 to the pattern from step 1, finishing the center block.

5. In order: sew the border to the left and right sides, and then to the top and bottom of the block from step 4. The top piece is complete.

6. Draw the quilting lines. Layer back fabric, batting, and quilt top piece. Baste, then quilt.

7. Trim the extra back fabric and batting to the edges of the top piece. Wrap the perimeter with the 1⅜" (3.5 cm) -wide binding fabric to finish.

Quilt Diagram

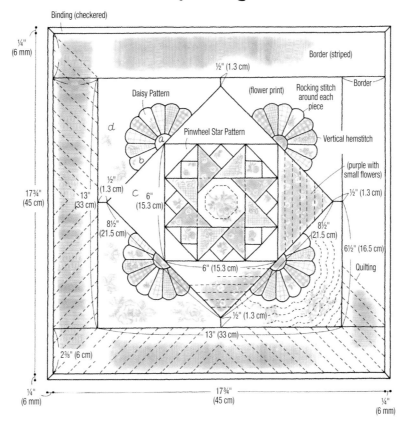

One of each: Front Fabric (Patchwork), Batting, Back Fabric (Print)

Cut pieces with a ¼" (6 mm) seam allowance.

Prepare 21⅝" × 21⅝" (55 × 55 cm) of the back fabric and batting.

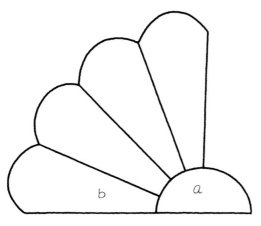

Full-size Daisy Pattern

Cut pieces with a ¼" (6 mm) seam allowance.

Larger Quilts

Month-by-Month Quilt I

Quilt on page 37
Finished Dimensions 70⅝" × 57⅝" (179.4 × 143.4 cm)
Pattern and quilting design: side B (see insert)

Materials

COTTON FABRIC

Border Pattern a (border, Lattice B)	43⁵⁄₁₆" × 57⅝" (110 × 145 cm)
Border Pattern b (Lattice A)	43⁵⁄₁₆" × 19¹¹⁄₁₆" (110 × 50 cm)
Print (back fabric)	43⁵⁄₁₆" × 3.7 yd (110 × 340 cm)
Checkered print (binding)	43⁵⁄₁₆" × 11¹³⁄₁₆" (110 × 30 cm)

BATTING

Batting (thin)	1.7 yd × 2.1 yd (155 × 190 cm)

HEAVYWEIGHT YARN

White (for trapunto)	40 g

Cutting measurements for borders and binding are on the Quilt Diagrams.

Patchwork Quilting Terms

Piece

A single piece of fabric such as a triangle, square, or diamond.

Piecework · Piecing

Sewing together pieces such as triangles, squares, and diamonds.

Block

A collection of pieces sewn together into one contiguous shape.

Pattern

A design made up of patchwork.

Lattice

Strips of fabric sewn between blocks, creating sashing.

Border

Fabric sewn around a central quilt block like a frame.

Quilt Top

The decorative side of a quilt sewn from fabric with various techniques such as piecing and appliqué.

Quilting

Sewing together the three layers of a quilt: quilt top, batting, and back fabric.

Binding

Bias-weave or straight-grain fabric used for wrapping around and finishing the edges of a quilt.

Quilt Diagram

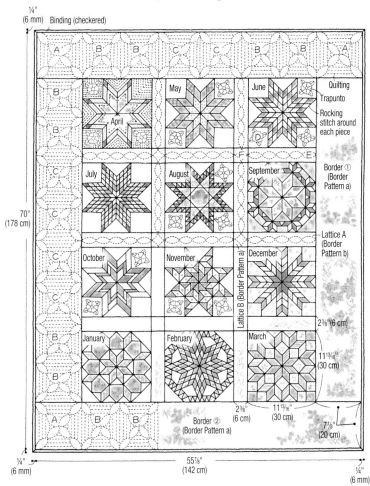

One of each: Front Fabric (Patchwork), Batting, Back Fabric (Print)

Cut the border and lattice leaving a ¼" (6 mm) seam allowance.

Prepare 1.7 yd × 2.1 yd (155 × 190 cm) of the batting and 2.4 yd × 1.8 yd (218 × 170 cm) of the back fabric.

GUIDE TO 12 PATTERNS

April	Virginia Star
May	Morning Star
June	Harvest Sun
July	Star of Bethlehem
August	Radiant Star
September	Star and Wreath Block
October	Connecticut Star
November	Flying Swallow
December	Christmas Star
January	Carpenter's Wheel
February	Shining Star
March	Broken Star

1. Make the quilt top

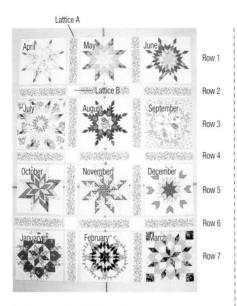

1 Arrange the 12 Star Patterns, Lattice A, and Lattice B to form the blocks for the seven rows.

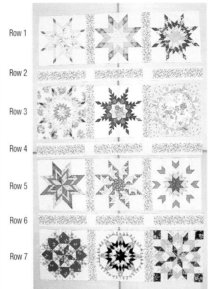

2 Sew the blocks for Rows 1, 3, 5, and 7. Alternate the three patterns with Lattice A, then sew together side by side using an outline satin stitch. Let the seam allowance fall to the side of the lattice. Next, sew together the blocks for Rows 2, 4, and 6. Alternate Lattice A and Lattice B, then sew together using an outline satin stitch. Let the seam allowance fall to the side of Lattice A. The blocks for Rows 1–7 are now complete.

3 Sew together the blocks for Rows 1–7. Sew together from edge to edge, letting the seam allowance fall to the sides of the blocks for Rows 2, 4, and 6. The center block is now complete.

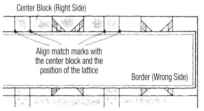

4 Cut Borders ① and ② so the flower print of Border Pattern a is centered (see page 135). Using a marking pen, make match marks on the back of Border ① in line with both the left and right sides of the patterns of the center block, and the positioning of the lattice. Assemble and center the Border ① on the right side of the center block, aligning the match marks with the center block patterns and lattice positions. Insert pins to mark.

5 Using a running stitch and working from edge to edge, sew together the block and Border ①. Sew the other Border ① to the other side (①). Let the seam allowance fall to the side of the border. Make the match marks on Border ② in the same way as in step 4. Center them at the top and bottom of the front side of the center block and align the match marks. Sew together from edge to edge using a running stitch (②). Let the seam allowance fall to the side of the border. Using an iron, press the entire piece. The quilt top piece is now complete.

2. Draw the quilting lines

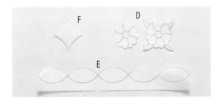

1 Using thick tracing paper, transfer the quilting line patterns. Make two copies of paper Pattern D: one for the design outline (right side) and one for the inside design lines (left side). For the paper Pattern E (for Lattice A), cut out one side so it is easier to transfer. For the paper Pattern F (for Lattice B), make as shown in the design.

2 Copy Design D anywhere within the pattern. Copy and trace the right side pattern from step 1 with a marking pen.

3 Align the left side pattern with the outline from step 2, then draw the inside design lines.

4 Finish creating the design lines freehand.

5 Using the right angle of a triangular ruler, mark along the outside of the flower design at ½" (1 cm) intervals.

6 Place Pattern E over Lattice A and copy the curved design. Next, flip the pattern over and copy the other side of the curved pattern.

7 For Pattern F, center the pointed sides on Lattice B, then trace the outline.

8 Free-draw a design into each pattern. See the quilt diagram on page 70 for sewing the border, and draw Designs A, B, and C.

3. Baste and quilt

If you cannot find batting large enough, bind together two pieces of batting to the proper dimensions.

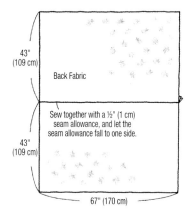

43" (109 cm)

Back Fabric

Sew together with a ½" (1 cm) seam allowance, and let the seam allowance fall to one side.

43" (109 cm)

67" (170 cm)

1 Prepare the 2.4 yd × 1.8 yd (218 × 170 cm) back fabric by sewing as shown in the diagram.

2 Spread out the back fabric onto a flat working surface (with the wrong side facing up) and tack down on the four sides. Next, center and layer the batting and the quilt top piece, tacking them down on four sides so the three layers of fabric do not slide. See page 72 for complete quilting instructions. Baste.

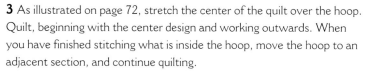

Quilting Order

1. Quilt the center of the pattern.
2. Rocking stitch around the pieces.
3. Quilt the lattice.
4. Rocking stitch around the lattice.
5. Quilt the border.

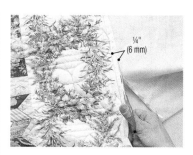

¼" (6 mm)

3 As illustrated on page 72, stretch the center of the quilt over the hoop. Quilt, beginning with the center design and working outwards. When you have finished stitching what is inside the hoop, move the hoop to an adjacent section, and continue quilting.

4 When the quilting is finished, remove the basting. Leaving a ¼" (6 mm) seam allowance, trim extra front fabric, batting, and back fabric.

4. Wrap the perimeter of the quilt with binding fabric and finish

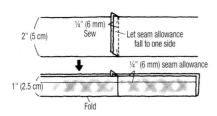

1 Cut out the checkered fabric (straight grain) into 2" (5 cm) -wide pieces. Join them to make a 7 yd (640 cm) strip. Fold in half (right side out) and mark a sewing line ¼" (6 mm) inside the edge.

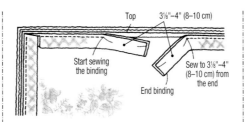

2 See page 74 for how to sew the binding around the perimeter. Toward the end of the binding, sew to about 3⅛"–4" (8–10 cm) before the start of the binding. Leave a ¼" (6 mm) seam allowance for the binding (when joined to the beginning of the binding). Trim extra.

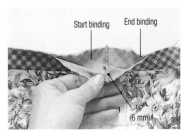

3 Sew the ends of the binding into a fold at the ¼" (6 mm) seam allowance. Let the seam allowance fall to one side.

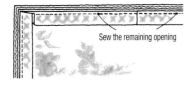

4 Fold the binding in half and align with the rest. Sew up the remaining opening.

5 Fold the binding over to the back side, align the fold with the sewing line, and set with pins. Fold the corners into a frame. Using a vertical hemstitch, sew the folded section by pricking the needle just along the edge of the seam. Do not hemstitch the frame sections. Wash the quilt to remove the marking pen (see page 75).

5. Add the trapunto

See pages 104–105 for trapunto instructions.

Add the trapunto to the Flower Design D. Double thread a trapunto needle with heavy white yarn. First, pass the yarn through the flower petals on the back fabric side of the quilt. Pass the yarn through four times, aligning each strand of yarn. Finish all flower petals this way. Next, pass the yarn four times through the flower centers, and then through the leaves. For the leaves, pass the yarn through from root to tip. Then make two passes on both the left and the right side. The quilt is finished.

Mini-Quilts

Mini Month-by-Month Quilt

Quilt on page 36
Finished size 35⅝" × 28½" (90.4 × 72.4 cm)

For the miniature quilt, reduce the measurements of Month-by-Month Quilt I by half, and create it in the same color scheme. The sewing instructions are the same as for the full-size Month-by-Month Quilt.

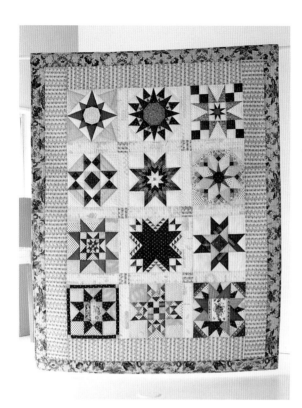

Month-by-Month Quilt II

Quilt on page 38
Finished Dimensions 70⅝" × 57⅝" (179.4 × 143.4 cm)
Pattern: side B (see insert)

Materials

COTTON FABRIC

Checkered (several styles) (pieces)	as needed
Natural print (Lattice A)	43⁵⁄₁₆" × 23⅝" (110 × 60 cm)
Blue print (Lattice B, C, and D)	43⁵⁄₁₆" × 39½" (110 × 100 cm)
Flower print (Border A and B, binding fabric)	43⁵⁄₁₆" × 39½" (110 × 100 cm)
Print (back fabric)	43⁵⁄₁₆" × 3.5 y (110 × 320 cm)

BATTING

Batting	2.2 yd × 1.75 yd (200 × 160 cm)

Cutting measurements for borders and binding are on the Quilt Diagrams.

Instructions

1. Sewing with piecework, make Patterns ① – ⑫.

2. Referring to the Month-by-Month Quilt instructions on page 134, create the quilt top piece.

3. Draw the quilting lines. Layer the back fabric, batting, and quilt top piece. Baste, then quilt.

4. Trim extra back fabric and batting to the edges of the top piece. Wrap the perimeter with 1⅜ (3.5 cm) -wide binding fabric to finish.

Quilt Diagram

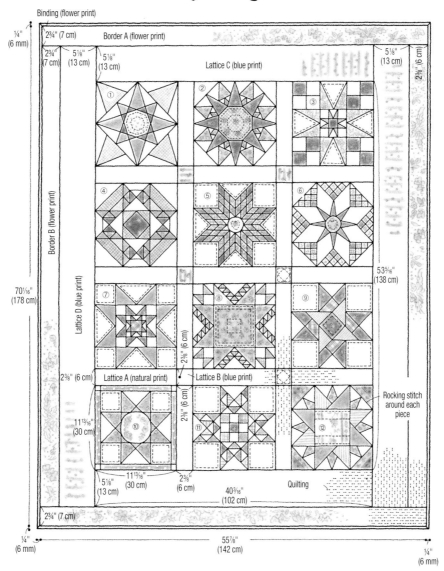

One layer each: Front Fabric (Patchwork), Batting, Back Fabric (Print)

Cut out pieces leaving a ¼" (6 mm) seam allowance.

Prepare 2.2 yd × 1.75 yd (200 × 160 cm) for the back fabric and batting.

Larger Quilts

Eight-Point Star

Quilt on page 42
Finished Dimensions 2.1 yd × 1.6 yd (191.8 × 149.4 cm)
Paper pattern and quilting design: side B (see insert)

Materials

COTTON FABRIC

Print (several colors, pieces)	as needed
Checkered print (Piece b, lattice)	43⁵⁄₁₆" × 43⁵⁄₁₆" (110 × 110 cm)
Wine colored (bias fabric for binding)	1" × 7.6 yd (2.5 × 700 cm)
Print (back fabric)	43⁵⁄₁₆" × 3.7 yd (110 × 340 cm)

BATTING

Batting	43⁵⁄₁₆" × 3.7 yd (110 × 340 cm)

CORD

Cord (for binding)	³⁄₁₆" (5 mm) thick, 7.6 yd (700 cm)

HEAVYWEIGHT YARN

White (for trapunto)	as needed

Cutting measurements for borders and binding are on the Quilt Diagrams.

Instructions

1. Make 20 Eight-Point Star Patterns. Sew these together with the 12 square b Pieces and the triangular pieces to form the center block.

2. Around the quilt block, sew the lattice and borders (which are pieced together) to finish the quilt top piece.

3. Draw the quilting lines. Layer the back fabric, batting, and quilt top piece. Baste, then quilt, leaving about ⅛" (3 mm) around the outside.

4. Trim extra back fabric and batting.

5. Referring to the diagram on the facing page, make the binding cord. Insert the binding cord between the quilt top and batting layers. Sew the two layers (not the back fabric) together along one edge using a running stitch.

6. Move the binding cord to the outside. Fold over the back fabric and finish the seam with a hemstitch.

7. Finish the quilting remaining from step 3.

8. Wash the quilt (see page 75). When dry, add the trapunto (see pages 104–105).

Quilt Diagram

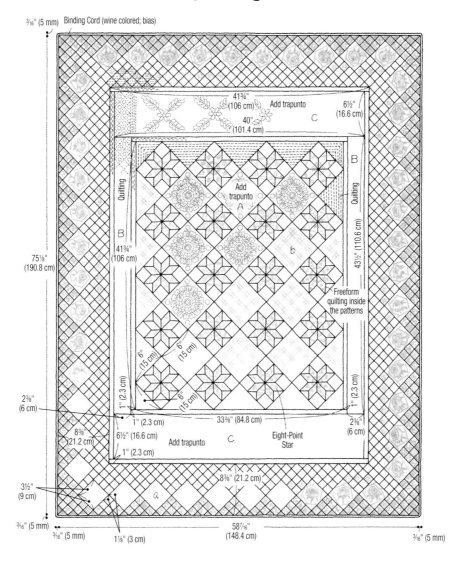

One layer each: Front Fabric (Patchwork), Batting, Back Fabric (Print)

Cut pieces leaving a ¼" (6 mm) seam allowance.

Prepare 43⁵⁄₁₆ yd × 3.7 yd (110 × 340 cm) of the back fabric and batting.

Making the Binding Cord

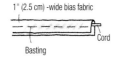

1" (2.5 cm) -wide bias fabric

Cord

Basting

Sewing Border Block a

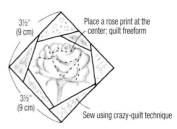

3½" (9 cm)

Place a rose print at the center; quilt freeform

3½" (9 cm)

Sew using crazy-quilt technique

Florida Star

Quilt on page 30
Finished Dimensions 82½" × 58" (209.4 × 147.4 cm)
Pattern: side A (see insert)

Materials

COTTON FABRIC

Various prints (pieces, lattice)	as needed
Green print (lattice, border, binding)	43⁵⁄₁₆" × 2.2 yd (110 × 200 cm)
Print (back fabric)	43⁵⁄₁₆" × 5 yd (110 × 460 cm)

BATTING

Batting	90½" × 39½" (230 × 165 cm)

Cutting measurements for borders and binding are on the Quilt Diagrams.

Instructions

1. Make 102 of the Florida Star Pattern (see page 102) in several different colors.

2. Referring to the quilt diagram, make six rows, each consisting of 17 of the blocks from step 1 joined vertically. Sew the six rows together to form the quilt block.

3. Sew Lattice a to the left and right sides of the block.

4. Sew Lattice a and b together, and Lattice c and d together. Then fit the lattices to the block from step 3 and sew together.

5. Take the block from step 4 and sew Border A to the left and right sides, and Border B to the top and bottom. The quilt top piece is finished.

6. Draw the quilting lines. Layer the back fabric, batting, and quilt top piece. Baste, then quilt.

7. Trim any extra back fabric and batting to the edges of the top piece. Wrap the perimeter with the 1⅜" (3.5 cm) -wide binding fabric to finish.

Quilt Diagram

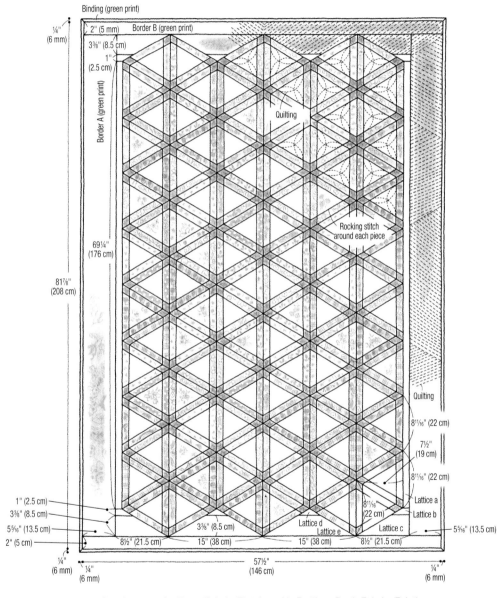

Binding (green print)

2" (5 mm) Border B (green print)

3⅜" (8.5 cm)

1" (2.5 cm)

¼" (6 mm)

Border A (green print)

Quilting

Rocking stitch around each piece

69¼" (176 cm)

81⅞" (208 cm)

Quilting

8¹¹⁄₁₆" (22 cm)

7½" (19 cm)

8¹¹⁄₁₆" (22 cm)

8¹¹⁄₁₆" (22 cm)

Lattice a

Lattice b

Lattice d

Lattice e

Lattice c

1" (2.5 cm)

3⅜" (8.5 cm)

5⁵⁄₁₆" (13.5 cm)

2" (5 cm)

¼" (6 mm)

8½" (21.5 cm)   15" (38 cm)   3⅜" (8.5 cm)   15" (38 cm)   8½" (21.5 cm)

5⁵⁄₁₆" (13.5 cm)

57½" (146 cm)

¼" (6 mm)   ¼" (6 mm)   ¼" (6 mm)

One layer each: Front Fabric (Patchwork), Batting, Back Fabric (Print)

Cut pieces leaving a ¼" (6 mm) seam allowance.

Prepare 90½" × 39½" (230 × 165 cm) of the back fabric and batting.

Castle Wall

Quilt on page 14
Finished Dimensions 73⅜" × 51¾" (186.4 × 131.4 cm)
Patterns: side A (see insert)

Materials

COTTON FABRIC

Various prints (pieces)	as needed
Red print (Piece b, pattern center piece)	43⁵⁄₁₆" × 2.2 yd (110 cm × 2 m)
Dark red (Piece a, pattern center piece)	43⁵⁄₁₆" × 19¹¹⁄₁₆" (110 × 50 cm)
Red woven pattern (binding)	43⁵⁄₁₆" × 11¹³⁄₁₆" (110 × 30 cm)
Print (back fabric)	43⁵⁄₁₆" × 3.3 yd (110 × 300 cm)

BATTING

Batting	80¾" × 59" (205 × 150 cm)

HEAVYWEIGHT YARN

White (for trapunto)	as needed

Cutting measurements for borders and binding are on the Quilt Diagrams.

Instructions

1. Make patterns ①, ②, and ③.

2. Alternate four of Pattern ③ with three of Piece a, and sew them together side by side. Sew Piece b to the top and bottom of the block to form the lattice.

3. Alternate three of Pattern ② with two of the lattice from step 2 and sew together side by side. Make four rows of this Block A.

4. Alternate Pattern ① and the lattice from step 2 and sew together. Make three rows of this Block B.

5. Referring to the quilt diagram, arrange Block A and Block B and sew together to form the quilt top piece.

6. Draw the quilting lines. Layer the back fabric, batting, and quilt top piece. Baste, then quilt.

7. Trim extra back fabric and batting to the edges of the top piece. Wrap the perimeter with 1⅜" (3.5 cm) -wide binding fabric to finish. Wash the quilt. When dry, add the trapunto (see pages 104–105).

Quilt Diagram

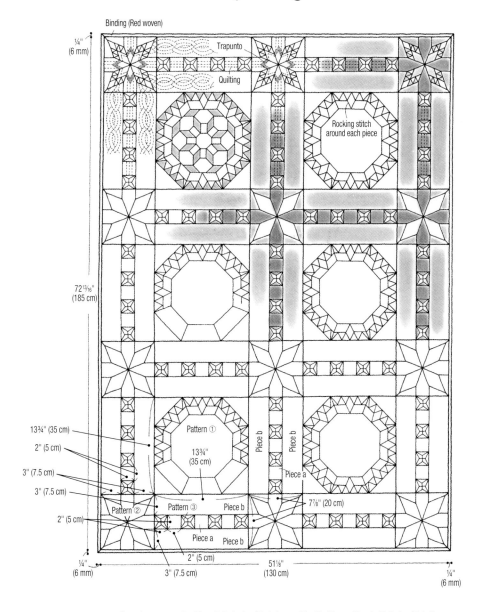

One layer each: Front Fabric (Patchwork), Batting, Back Fabric (Print)

Cut pieces leaving a ¼" (6 mm) seam allowance.

Prepare 80¾" × 59" (205 × 150 cm) of the back fabric and batting.

Sunburst

Quilt on page 28
Finished Dimensions 76⅜" × 61" (194 × 155 cm)
Pattern: side C (see insert)

Materials

COTTON FABRIC

Twelve different prints (stripes, dots, flowers, etc) (pieces, binding fabric)	as needed
Print (back fabric)	43⁵⁄₁₆" × 3.7 yd (110 × 340 cm)

BATTING

Batting	2.3 yd × 1.8 yd (210 × 170 cm)

Cutting measurements for borders and binding are on the Quilt Diagrams.

Instructions

1. Sew together all pieces to form the quilt top (refer to the diagram).

2. Layer the back fabric, batting, and quilt top and baste.

3. Quilt, using a rocking stitch around each piece. Trim extra back fabric and batting to the edges of the top piece.

4. Cut the binding fabric to 1⅜" (3.5 cm) wide and 7.9 yd (720 cm) long. Wrap it around the perimeter of the quilt to create a ¼" (6 mm) -wide border and finish.

Quilt Diagram

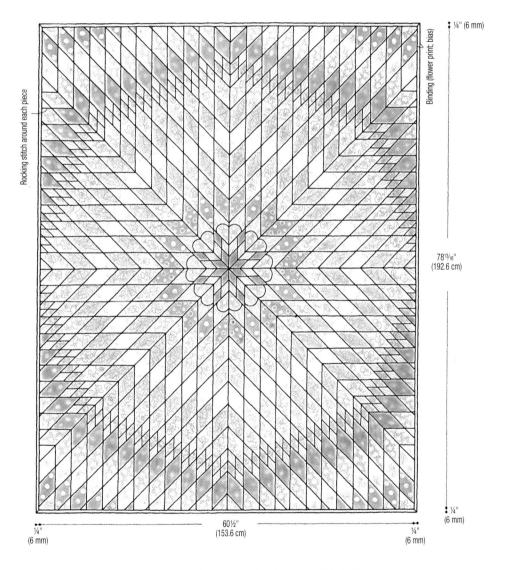

One layer each: Front Fabric (Patchwork), Batting, Back Fabric (Print)

Cut pieces leaving a ¼" (6 mm) seam allowance.

Prepare 2.3 yd × 1.8 yd (210 × 170 cm) of the back fabric and batting.

Larger Quilts

Star and Wreath Block

Quilt on page 26

Finished Dimensions 86³⁄₁₆" × 74³⁄₁₆" (218.8 × 188.4 cm)

Patterns: side C for Quilt Pattern A and side D for Quilt Pattern B (full size, see insert)

Materials

COTTON FABRIC

Five different orange (solids and prints, pieces)	as needed
White (border)	43⁵⁄₁₆" × 4 yd (110 × 370 cm)
Green print (border)	9⅞" × 2.2 yd (25 × 200 cm)
Print (back fabric)	43⁵⁄₁₆" × 5 yd (110 × 470 cm)

BATTING

Batting	92½" × 80¾" (235 × 205 cm)

HEAVYWEIGHT YARN

White (for trapunto)	as needed

Cutting measurements for borders and binding are on the Quilt Diagrams.

Instructions

1. Draw the appliqué design around the center hexagon, then add the appliqué.

2. Sew together the pieces to make the quilt top.

3. Draw the quilting lines in as you like. Layer the back fabric, batting, and quilt top piece. Baste.

4. Quilt. Trim extra back fabric and batting to the edges of the top piece.

5. To finish the quilt: fold the seam allowance three times to the backside of the quilt and finish with a hemstitch.

6. Wash the quilt (see page 75). When it is dry, add the trapunto (see pages 104–105).

Quilt Diagram

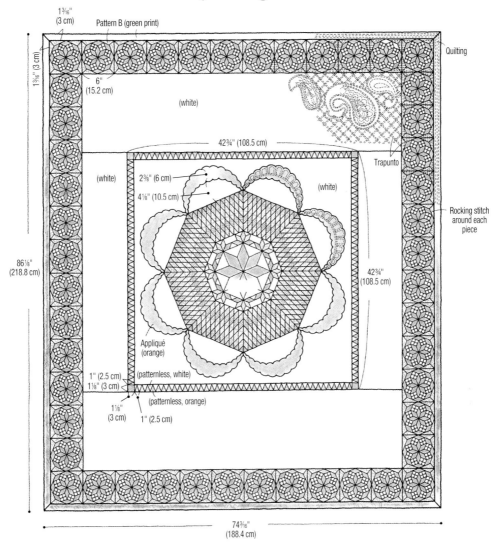

1³⁄₁₆" (3 cm)

Pattern B (green print)

Quilting

1³⁄₁₆" (3 cm)

6" (15.2 cm)

(white)

(white)

42¾" (108.5 cm)

Trapunto

2³⁄₈" (6 cm)

(white)

86⅛" (218.8 cm)

4⅛" (10.5 cm)

Rocking stitch around each piece

42¾" (108.5 cm)

Appliqué (orange)

1" (2.5 cm)

1⅛" (3 cm)

(patternless, white)

1⅛" (3 cm)

(patternless, orange)

1" (2.5 cm)

74³⁄₁₆" (188.4 cm)

One layer each: Front Fabric (Patchwork), Batting, Back Fabric (Print)

Cut pieces leaving a ¼" (6 mm) seam allowance. Leave a ⅛" (3 mm) allowance for appliqué and ⅝" (1.5 cm) around the outside of the border.

Prepare 92½" × 80¾" (235 × 205 cm) of the back fabric and batting.

Larger Quilts

Rising Star

Quilt on page 57
Finished Dimensions 67½" × 67½" (171.4 × 171.4 cm)
Pattern: side C (see insert)

Materials

COTTON FABRIC

Red flower (pieces)	43⁵⁄₁₆" × 15¾" (110 × 40 cm)
White flower (pieces)	43⁵⁄₁₆" × 11¾" (110 × 30 cm)
Orange flower (pieces)	43⁵⁄₁₆" × 11¾" (110 × 30 cm)
Blue border (border, binding fabric)	43⁵⁄₁₆" × 3.8 yd (110 × 350 cm)
Light green dot print (pieces)	43⁵⁄₁₆" × 19¹¹⁄₁₆" (110 × 50 cm)
Beige print (lattice)	43⁵⁄₁₆" × 23½" (110 × 60 cm)
Print (back fabric)	43⁵⁄₁₆" × 4.2 yd (110 × 380 cm)

BATTING

Batting	2.1 yd × 2.1 yd (190 × 190 cm)

HEAVYWEIGHT YARN

White (for trapunto)	as needed

Cutting measurements for borders and binding are on the Quilt Diagrams.

Instructions

1. Sew together the pieces to form the quilt top (see quilt diagram).

2. Draw the quilting lines. Layer the back fabric, batting, and quilt top piece. Baste.

3. Quilt. For the red flower print and the blue border pieces, use a shadow quilt stitch (with quilt thread that matches the fabric). Trim extra back fabric and batting to the edges of the top piece.

4. Cut the binding fabric to 1⅜" (3.5 cm) wide and 7.9 yd (720 cm) long. Wrap it around the perimeter of the quilt to create a ¼" (6 mm) -wide border and finish.

5. Wash the quilt (see page 75). When it is dry, add the trapunto (see pages 104–105).

Quilt Diagram

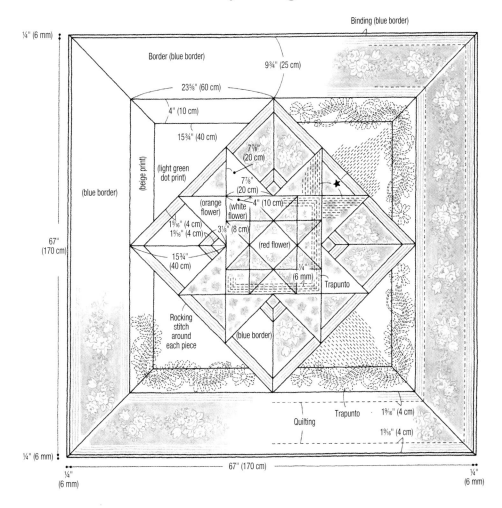

Binding (blue border)

¼" (6 mm)

Border (blue border)

9¾" (25 cm)

23⅝" (60 cm)

4" (10 cm)

15¾" (40 cm)

(beige print)

(light green dot print)

7⅞" (20 cm)

7⅞" (20 cm)

(orange flower)

(white flower)

4" (10 cm)

(blue border)

1⁹⁄₁₆" (4 cm)
1⁹⁄₁₆" (4 cm)

3⅛" (8 cm)

(red flower)

15¾" (40 cm)

¼" (6 mm)

Trapunto

67" (170 cm)

Rocking stitch around each piece

(blue border)

Quilting

Trapunto

1⁹⁄₁₆" (4 cm)

1⁹⁄₁₆" (4 cm)

¼" (6 mm)

67" (170 cm)

¼" (6 mm)

¼" (6 mm)

One layer each: Front Fabric (Patchwork), Batting, Back Fabric (Print)

Cut pieces leaving a ¼" (6 mm) seam allowance.

Prepare 2.1 yd × 2.1 yd (190 × 190 cm) of the back fabric and batting.

★ Quilting stitch guide

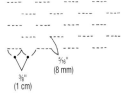

⅝" (8 mm)

⅜" (1 cm)

Ten-Point Star

Quilt on page 56
Finished Dimensions 53⁵⁄₁₆" × 53⁵⁄₁₆" (135.4 × 135.4 cm)
Pattern: side C (see insert)

Materials

COTTON FABRIC

Eleven to twelve different fabrics (checkered, dotted, flower, etc) (pieces)	as needed
Light purple (solid) and light purple (checkered print) (pieces)	43⁵⁄₁₆" × 23⅝" (110 × 60 cm)
Flower pattern (border)	19¹¹⁄₁₆" × 55" (50 × 140 cm)
Light purple (striped; binding fabric)	43⁵⁄₁₆" × 19¹¹⁄₁₆" (110 × 50 cm)
Print (back fabric)	43⁵⁄₁₆" × 3.4 yd (110 × 310 cm)

BATTING

Batting	61" × 61" (155 × 155 cm)

HEAVYWEIGHT YARN

White (for trapunto)	as needed

Cutting measurements for borders and binding are on the Quilt Diagrams.

Instructions

1. Sew pieces together to make the circular center block (see quilt diagram).

2. Around the outside of the circular block, sew on the solid and checkered light purple pieces.

3. Sew on the border to complete the quilt top piece.

4. Draw the quilting lines. Layer the back fabric, batting, and quilt top piece.

5. Quilt. Trim extra back fabric and batting to the edges of the top piece.

6. Prepare 6 yd (550 cm) of the 1⅜" (3.5 cm) -wide binding fabric. Wrap it around the perimeter of the quilt to create a ¼" (6 mm) -wide border and finish.

7. Wash the quilt (see page 75). When it is dry, add the trapunto (see pages 104–105).

Quilt Diagram

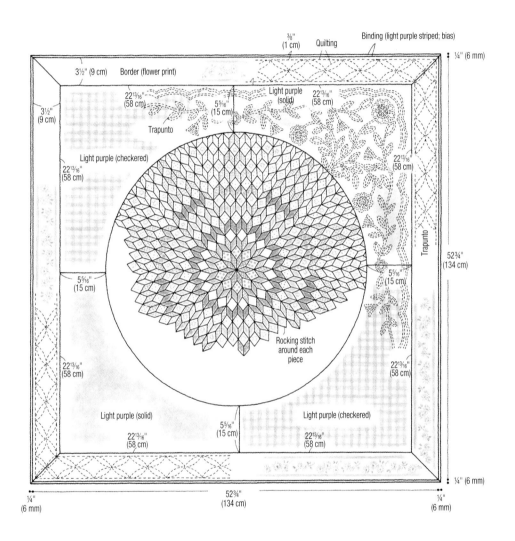

One layer each: Front Fabric (Patchwork), Batting, Back Fabric (Print)

Cut pieces leaving a ¼" (6 mm) seam allowance.

Prepare 61" × 61" (155 × 155 cm) of the back fabric and batting.

Lone Star

Quilt on page 20
Finished Dimensions 75⅜" × 59⅝" (191.4 × 151.4 cm)
Pattern and quilting design: side C (see insert)

Materials

COTTON FABRIC

Five to six varied dark colors, Eleven to twelve varied light colors (pieces)	as needed
Beige checkered (border, binding fabric)	43⁵⁄₁₆" × 1.75 yd (110 × 160 cm)
Beige flower (border)	43⁵⁄₁₆" × 9⅞" (110 × 25 cm)
Print (back fabric)	43⁵⁄₁₆" × 3.7 yd (110 × 340 cm)

BATTING

Batting	2.3 yd × 1.8 yd (210 × 170 cm)

HEAVYWEIGHT YARN

White (for trapunto)	as needed

Cutting measurements for borders and binding are on the Quilt Diagrams.

Instructions

1. Sew together pieces and make 90 of Pattern A (see page 84). Cut out 89 of Piece a from the light-colored fabrics.

2. Sew together the center block. Around the block, alternate Pattern A and Piece a and sew together.

3. To finish the quilt top piece, sew the borders around the block from step 2.

4. Draw the quilting lines. Layer the back fabric, batting, and quilt front piece. Baste.

5. Quilt, and then trim extra back fabric and batting to the edges of the top piece.

6. Cut the binding fabric to 1⅜" (3.5 cm) wide and 7.6 yd (700 cm) long. Wrap it around the perimeter of the quilt to create a ¼" (6 mm) wide border and finish.

7. Wash the quilt (see page 75). When it is dry, add the trapunto (see pages 104–105).

Quilt Diagram

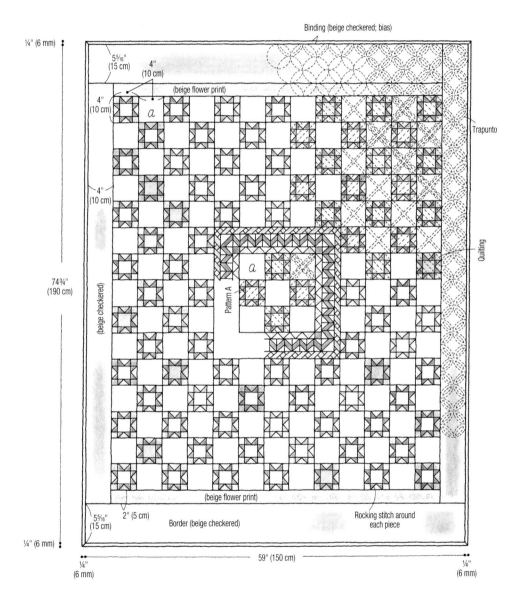

One layer each: Front Fabric (Patchwork), Batting, Back Fabric (Print)

Cut pieces leaving a ¼" (6 mm) seam allowance.

Prepare 2.3 yd × 1.8 yd (210 × 170 cm) of the back fabric and batting.

Larger Quilts

Feathered-Edge Star of Bethlehem

Quilt on page 46
Finished Dimensions 67¾" × 67¾" (172.2 × 172.2 cm)
Full-size pattern: side D (see insert)

Materials

COTTON FABRIC

Eleven different types of flower prints (Pieces a, e)	as needed
White flower (Piece b, c, d)	43⁵⁄₁₆" × 59" (110 × 150 cm)
Dark brown dot print (Piece b, binding cord)	43⁵⁄₁₆" × 23⅝" (110 × 60 cm)
Dark brown flower print (Piece e)	43⁵⁄₁₆" × 39½" (110 × 100 cm)
Print (back fabric)	43⁵⁄₁₆" × 4.2 yd (110 × 380 cm)

BATTING

Batting	2.1 yd × 2.1 yd (190 × 190 cm)

CORD

Cord (for binding)	¹⁄₁₆" (1.5 mm) thick, 7.6 yd (700 cm)

Cutting measurements for borders and binding are on the Quilt Diagrams.

Instructions

1. Sew together Pieces a, b, c, and d to form the center block.

2. Sew together e Pieces and then join that with the block from step 1 to make the top piece.

3. Draw the quilting lines. Arrange the back fabric, batting, and top piece in three layers and baste.

4. Quilt the pieces except for one row along the outside. Trim any extra back fabric and batting in line with the top piece.

5. Prepare 7.6 yd (700 cm) length of the 1" (2.5 cm) -wide binding cord fabric. Fold the width in half and insert the cord, then see page 142 for instructions and apply the binding cord.

6. Line up and center the binding cord with the finishing line of the top piece, and then sew together leaving out the back fabric.

7. Flip the binding cord to the front, and then fold the back fabric and hemstitch to finish.

8. Quilt over the unfinished sections from step 4.

Quilt Diagram

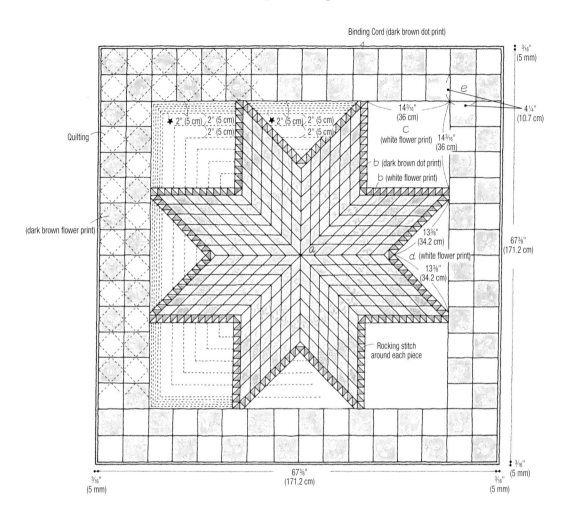

Binding Cord (dark brown dot print)

³⁄₁₆" (5 mm)

e

4¼" (10.7 cm)

14³⁄₁₆" (36 cm)

c (white flower print)

14³⁄₁₆" (36 cm)

2" (5 cm) 2" (5 cm)
★ 2" (5 cm) 2" (5 cm)
2" (5 cm) 2" (5 cm)

b (dark brown dot print)

b (white flower print)

Quilting

a

13⅜" (34.2 cm)

d (white flower print)

13⅜" (34.2 cm)

(dark brown flower print)

67⅜" (171.2 cm)

Rocking stitch around each piece

³⁄₁₆" (5 mm)

³⁄₁₆" (5 mm)

67⅜" (171.2 cm)

³⁄₁₆" (5 mm)

³⁄₁₆" (5 mm)

One layer each: Front Fabric (Patchwork), Batting, Back Fabric (Print)

Cut pieces leaving a ¼" (6 mm) seam allowance.

Prepare 2.1 yd × 2.1 yd (190 × 190 cm) of the back fabric and batting.

★ Quilting stitch guide

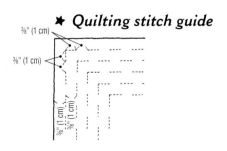

⅜" (1 cm)

⅜" (1 cm)

⅜" (1 cm)

⅜" (1 cm)

Tumbling Star

Quilt on page 48
Finished Dimensions 85¼" × 76" (213.2 × 190.2 cm)
Pattern: side C (see insert)

Materials

COTTON FABRIC

Golden brown flower print (pieces)	43⁵⁄₁₆" × 60" (110 × 150 cm)
Eighty fabric scraps (pieces)	as needed
Dark brown flower print (border, binding)	43⁵⁄₁₆" × 2.2 yd (110 × 200 cm)
Print (back fabric)	43⁵⁄₁₆" × 5 yd (110 × 460 cm)

BATTING

Batting	92" × 80¾" (230 × 205 cm)

HEAVYWEIGHT YARN

White (for trapunto)	as needed

Cutting measurements for borders and binding are on the Quilt Diagrams.

Instructions

1. Sew together the pieces and sew the border around the outside to form the top piece (see quilt diagram).

2. Draw the quilting lines. Layer the back fabric, batting, and quilt top piece. Baste.

3. Quilt, and then trim extra back fabric and batting to the edges of the top piece.

4. Cut the binding fabric to 1⅜" (3.5 cm) wide and 9 yd (820 cm) long. Wrap it around the perimeter of the quilt to create a ¼" (6 mm) -wide border and finish.

5. Wash the quilt (see page 75). When it is dry, add the trapunto (see pages 104–105).

160   CLASSIC QUILTS Contemporary Style

Quilt Diagram

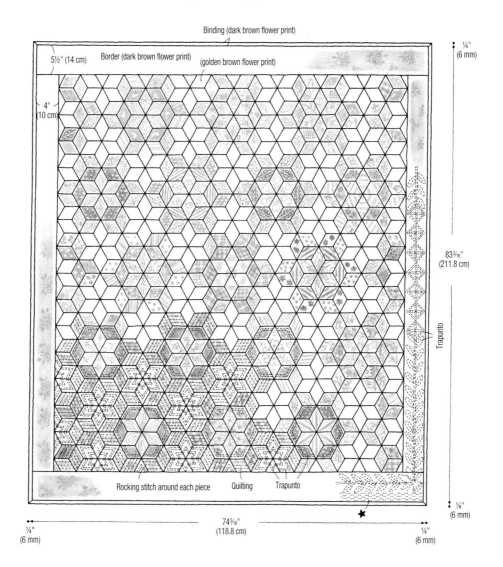

Binding (dark brown flower print)

Border (dark brown flower print)

(golden brown flower print)

5½" (14 cm)

¼" (6 mm)

4" (10 cm)

83³⁄₁₆" (211.8 cm)

Trapunto

Rocking stitch around each piece   Quilting   Trapunto

¼" (6 mm)

¼" (6 mm)

74⁵⁄₁₆" (118.8 cm)

¼" (6 mm)

¼" (6 mm)

One layer each: Front Fabric (Patchwork), Batting, Back Fabric (Print)

Cut pieces leaving a ¼" (6 mm) seam allowance.

Prepare 92" × 80¾" (230 × 205 cm) of the back fabric and batting.

❧ Quilting stitch guide

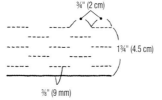

¾" (2 cm)

1¾" (4.5 cm)

⅜" (9 mm)

Round-Robin Quilts

Eight-Point Star

Quilt on page 25
Finished Dimensions 36½" × 36½" (91.4 × 91.4 cm)
Pattern and appliqué: side C (see insert)

Materials

COTTON FABRIC

Seven different prints (flowers, dots, etc.) (pieces)	as needed
Seven different prints (appliqué fabric)	as needed
Moss green dot print (border, binding fabric)	43⁵⁄₁₆" × 40" (110 × 100 cm)
Print (back fabric)	43⁵⁄₁₆" × 43⁵⁄₁₆" (110 × 110 cm)

BATTING

Batting	43⁵⁄₁₆" × 43⁵⁄₁₆" (110 × 110 cm)

Cutting measurements for borders and binding are on the Quilt Diagrams.

Instructions

1. Layout the border appliqué design, and then sew the appliqué.

2. Sew the pieces to form the quilt top.

3. Draw the quilting lines on the top piece.

4. Layer the back fabric, batting, and top piece. Baste.

5. Quilt, then trim extra back fabric and batting to the edges of the top piece.

6. Prepare four 38" (95 cm) lengths of the 1³⁄₈" (3.5 cm) -wide binding fabric. To finish the quilt, wrap the binding around the edges in the following order: left, right, top, and bottom.

Quilt Diagram

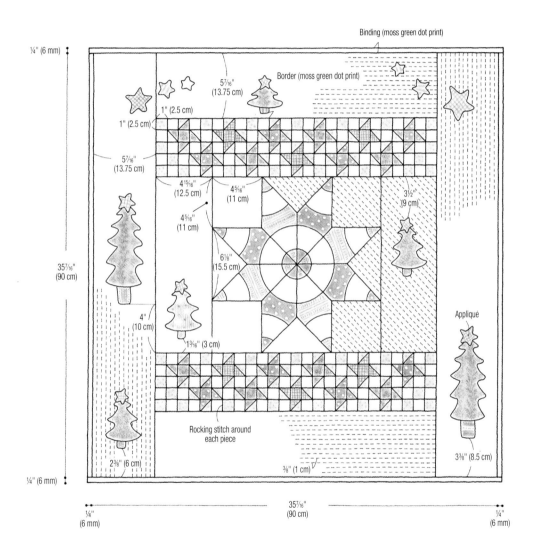

One layer each: Front Fabric (Patchwork), Batting, Back Fabric (Print)

Cut pieces leaving a ¼" (6 mm) seam allowance. Cut appliqué leaving a ⅛" (3 mm) seam allowance.

Prepare 43⁵⁄₁₆" × 43⁵⁄₁₆" (110 × 110 cm) of the back fabric and batting.

Round-Robin Quilts

Star of Bethlehem

Quilt on page 24
Finished Dimensions 37¼" × 37¼" (93 × 93 cm)
Pattern and appliqué: side C (see insert)

Materials

COTTON FABRIC

White snow print (pieces)	43⁵⁄₁₆" × 31½" (110 × 80 cm)
Beige flower print, green flower print, red flower print, solid red, green print, checkered, white snow print (pieces, appliqué fabric)	as needed
White print (pieces, border)	43⁵⁄₁₆" × 48" (110 × 120 cm)
Red star print (pieces, binding fabric)	43⁵⁄₁₆" × 40" (110 × 100 cm)
Holiday print (back fabric)	43⁵⁄₁₆" × 43⁵⁄₁₆" (110 × 110 cm)

BATTING

Batting	43⁵⁄₁₆" × 43⁵⁄₁₆" (110 × 110 cm)

Cutting measurements for borders and binding are on the Quilt Diagrams.

Instructions

1. Sew the border together into one piece.

2. Draw the appliqué design onto the center octagon shape and the border, then add the appliqué.

3. Sew the pieces and the border together to form the quilt top piece.

4. Draw the quilting lines. Layer the back fabric, batting, and quilt top piece. Baste.

5. Quilt, and then trim extra back fabric and batting to the edges of the top piece.

6. Cut the binding fabric to 1⅜" (3.5 cm) wide and 4.3 yd (390 cm) long. Wrap it around the perimeter of the quilt to create a ¼" (6 mm) -wide border and finish.

Quilt Diagram

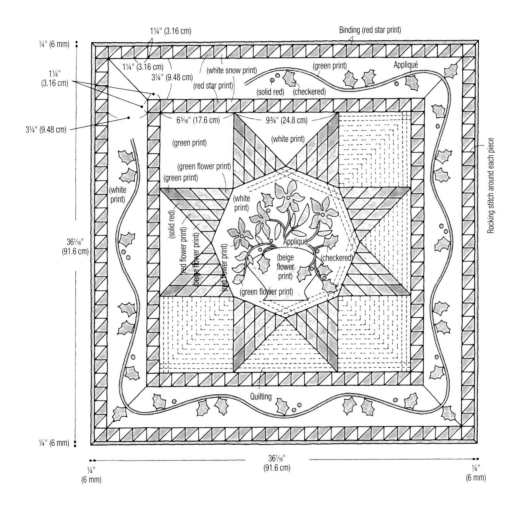

¼" (6 mm)

1¼" (3.16 cm)

Binding (red star print)

1¼" (3.16 cm)

1¼" (3.16 cm)
3¼" (9.48 cm)
(red star print)

(white snow print)

(green print)

Appliqué

(solid red)   (checkered)

3¼" (9.48 cm)

6⁵⁄₁₆" (17.6 cm)   9¾" (24.8 cm)

(green print)

(white print)

(green flower print)
(green print)

(white print)

(white print)

(solid red)

Appliqué

(beige flower print)

(checkered)

(red flower print)

(beige flower print)

(red flower print)

36¹⁄₁₆"
(91.6 cm)

(green flower print)

Rocking stitch around each piece

Quilting

¼" (6 mm)

36¹⁄₁₆"
(91.6 cm)

¼"
(6 mm)

¼"
(6 mm)

One layer each: Front Fabric (Patchwork), Batting, Back Fabric (Holiday Print)

Cut pieces leaving a ¼" (6 mm) seam allowance. Cut appliqué leaving a ⅛" (3 mm) seam allowance.

Prepare 43⁵⁄₁₆" × 43⁵⁄₁₆" (110 × 110 cm) of back fabric and batting.

Round-Robin Quilts

Morning Star

Quilt on page 23
Finished Dimensions 36½" × 36½" (91.4 × 91.4 cm)
Pattern and appliqué: side C (see insert)

Materials

COTTON FABRIC

Twelve to thirteen different flower prints (pieces)	as needed
Checkered print (lattice)	43⁵⁄₁₆" × 3⁵⁄₁₆" (110 × 10 cm)
Yellow-green dot print (border)	43⁵⁄₁₆" × 36" (110 × 90 cm)
Beige flower print (border, binding)	43⁵⁄₁₆" × 19¹¹⁄₁₆" (110 × 50 cm)
Two pink, green flower prints (appliqué fabric)	as needed
Print (back fabric)	43⁵⁄₁₆" × 43⁵⁄₁₆" (110 × 110 cm)

BATTING

Batting	43⁵⁄₁₆" × 43⁵⁄₁₆" (110 × 110 cm)

Cutting measurements for borders and binding are on the Quilt Diagrams.

Instructions

1. Sew pieces together and make the center block (see quilt diagram).

2. Sew the border together into one piece.

3. Draw the appliqué designs onto the border, and then sew the appliqué.

4. Place the lattice between the center block and border. Sew together to finish the quilt top piece.

5. Draw in the quilting lines. Layer the back fabric, batting, and quilt top piece. Baste.

6. Quilt, then trim extra back fabric and batting to the edges of the top piece.

7. Cut the binding fabric to 1⅜" (3.5 cm) wide and 4.2 yd (380 cm) long. Wrap it around the perimeter of the quilt to create a ¼" (6 mm) -wide border and finish.

Quilt Diagram

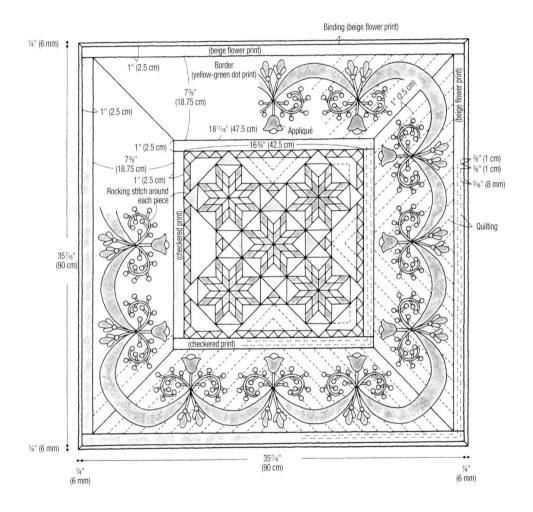

One layer each: Front Fabric (Patchwork), Batting, Back Fabric (Print)

Cut pieces leaving a ¼" (6 mm) seam allowance. Cut appliqué leaving a ⅛" (3 mm) seam allowance.

Prepare 43⁵⁄₁₆" × 43⁵⁄₁₆" (110 × 110 cm) of the back fabric and batting.

Ohio Star

Quilt on page 19
Finished Dimensions 36½" × 36½" (91.4 × 91.4 cm)
Full-size pattern and appliqué designs: side D (see insert)

Materials

COTTON FABRIC

Twenty different prints (flower, stripes, etc.) (pieces)	as needed
White flower print, green checkered print, green print (appliqué fabric)	as needed
Print (binding, back fabric)	43⁵⁄₁₆" × 52" (110 × 130 cm)

BATTING

Batting	43⁵⁄₁₆" × 43⁵⁄₁₆" (110 × 110 cm)

Cutting measurements for borders and binding are on the Quilt Diagrams.

Instructions

1. Sew the lattice together into one piece.

2. Draw the appliqué design onto the lattice and the center piece, and then sew the appliqué.

3. Make the center pattern and then sew to the lattice.

4. Sew squares together to form the Ohio Star Pattern (see page 78). Then sew that together with the block from step 2 to form the quilt top piece.

5. Layer the back fabric, batting, and top piece. Baste.

6. Quilt around each piece using a rocking stitch. Trim extra back fabric and batting to the edges of the top piece.

7. Cut the binding fabric to 1⅜" (3.5 cm) wide and 4.2 yd (380 cm) long. Wrap it around the perimeter of the quilt to create a ¼" (6 mm) -wide border and finish.

Quilt Diagram

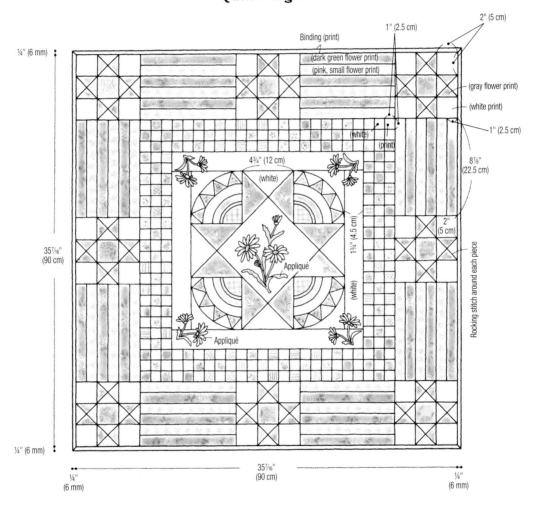

One layer each: Front Fabric (Patchwork), Batting, Back Fabric (Print)

Cut pieces leaving a ¼" (6 mm) seam allowance. Cut appliqué leaving a ⅛" (3 mm) seam allowance.

Prepare 43⁵⁄₁₆" × 43⁵⁄₁₆" (110 × 110 cm) of back fabric and batting.

Harvest Sun

Quilt on page 13
Finished Dimensions 36½" × 36½" (91.4 × 91.4 cm)
Full-size pattern and appliqué designs: side D (see insert).

Materials

COTTON FABRIC

Seven different prints (flower, striped, etc.) (pieces, binding fabric)	as needed
Checkered, small flower print (appliqué fabric)	as needed
Print (back fabric)	43⁵⁄₁₆" × 43⁵⁄₁₆" (110 × 110 cm)

BATTING

Batting	43⁵⁄₁₆" × 43⁵⁄₁₆" (110 × 110 cm)

Cutting measurements for borders and binding are on the Quilt Diagrams.

Instructions

1. Sew the border together into one piece. Position and draw the appliqué on the border and the pieces, then sew the appliqué.

2. Sew the border and the pieces together to form the quilt top piece.

3. Draw the quilting lines. Layer the back fabric, batting, and top piece. Baste.

4. Quilt, and then trim extra back fabric and batting to the edges of the top piece.

5. Cut the binding fabric to 1⅜" (3.5 cm) wide and 4.2 yd (380 cm) long. Wrap it around the perimeter of the quilt to create a ¼" (6 mm) -wide border and finish.

Quilt Diagram

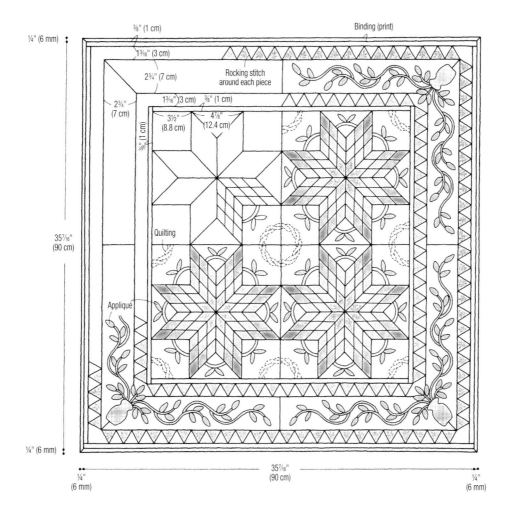

³⁄₈" (1 cm) Binding (print)

¼" (6 mm)

1³⁄₁₆" (3 cm)

2³⁄₄" (7 cm) Rocking stitch around each piece

2³⁄₄" (7 cm) 1³⁄₁₆" (3 cm) ³⁄₈" (1 cm)

3½" (8.8 cm) 4⁷⁄₈" (12.4 cm)

³⁄₈" (1 cm)

35⁷⁄₁₆" (90 cm)

Quilting

Appliqué

¼" (6 mm)

¼" (6 mm) 35⁷⁄₁₆" (90 cm) ¼" (6 mm)

One layer each: Front Fabric (Patchwork), Batting, Back Fabric (Print)

Cut pieces leaving a ¼" (6 mm) seam allowance. Cut appliqué leaving a ⅛" (3 mm) seam allowance.

Prepare 43⁵⁄₁₆" × 43⁵⁄₁₆" (110 × 110 cm) of the back fabric and batting.

Feathered Star

Quilt on page 10
Finished Dimensions 36½" × 36½" (91.4 × 91.4 cm)
Patterns A, B, and D: side D (see insert)
Pattern C: side A (see insert)

Materials

COTTON FABRIC

Light pink flower print, light pink small flower print, pink print, black small flower print, green print, green flower print (pieces, appliqué fabric)	as needed
Pink flower print (pieces, binding fabric)	43⁵⁄₁₆" × 43⁵⁄₁₆" (110 × 110 cm)
White print (pieces, border)	43⁵⁄₁₆" × 27½" (110 × 70 cm)
Print (back fabric)	43⁵⁄₁₆" × 43⁵⁄₁₆" (110 × 110 cm)

BATTING

Batting	43⁵⁄₁₆" × 43⁵⁄₁₆" (110 × 110 cm)

Cutting measurements for borders and binding are on the Quilt Diagrams.

Instructions

1. Sew the lattice together into one piece. Draw the appliqué designs, and draw the appliqué Patterns A and B, the lattice, and the border.

2. Make each pattern, then sew them together to form the top piece (see pages 76–77 for directions on how to make Pattern C).

3. Draw the quilting lines. Layer the back fabric, batting, and quilt top pieces. Baste.

4. Quilt, then trim extra back fabric and batting to the edges of the top piece.

5. Cut the binding fabric to 1⅜" (3.5 cm) wide and 4.2 yd (380 cm) long. Wrap it around the perimeter of the quilt to create a ¼" (6 mm) -wide border and finish.

Quilt Diagram

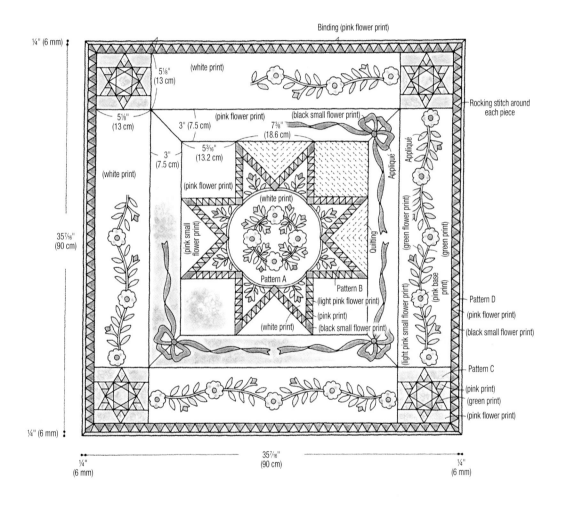

One layer each: Front Fabric (Patchwork), Batting, Back Fabric (Print)

Cut pieces leaving a ¼" (6 mm) seam allowance. Cut appliqué leaving a ⅛" (3 mm) seam allowance.

Prepare 43⁵⁄₁₆" × 43⁵⁄₁₆" (110 × 110 cm) of the back fabric and batting.

Tennessee Star

Quilt on page 11
Finished Dimensions 35¾" × 35¾" (89.4 × 89.4 cm)
Full-size pattern: side D (see insert)

Materials

COTTON FABRIC

Eight different prints (Piece a, flower, paisley, etc.)	as needed
Beige flower print (pieces)	43⁵⁄₁₆" × 15¾" (110 × 40 cm)
Green flower print (pieces)	43⁵⁄₁₆" × 15¾" (110 × 40 cm)
Red print (pieces)	43⁵⁄₁₆" × 11¹³⁄₁₆" (110 × 30 cm)
White flower print (pieces)	43⁵⁄₁₆" × 9⅞" (110 × 25 cm)
Pink flower print (lattice, border)	43⁵⁄₁₆" × 13¾" (110 × 35 cm)
Checkered print (binding fabric)	43⁵⁄₁₆" × 7⅞" (110 × 20 cm)
Print (back fabric)	43⁵⁄₁₆" × 43⁵⁄₁₆" (110 × 110 cm)

BATTING

Batting	43⁵⁄₁₆" × 43⁵⁄₁₆" (110 × 110 cm)

Cutting measurements for borders and binding are on the Quilt Diagrams.

Instructions

1. Make four of Pattern A and sew them together.

2. Make Pattern B and connect the squares. Then insert the lattice and sew together with the block from step 1. Next, sew the border to complete the quilt top piece.

3. Layer the back fabric, batting, and quilt top piece. Baste.

4. Quilt using a rocking stitch around each piece. Trim extra back fabric and batting to the edges of the top piece.

5. Cut the binding fabric to 1⅜" (3.5 cm) wide and 4.2 yd (380 cm) long. Wrap it around the perimeter of the quilt to create a ¼" (6 mm) -wide border and finish.

Quilt Diagram

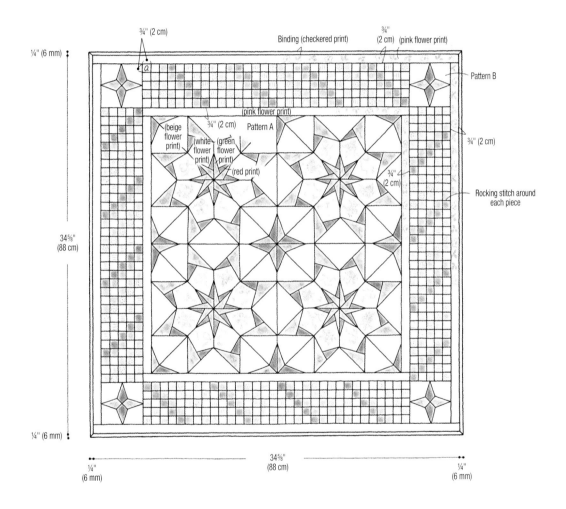

¾" (2 cm)

Binding (checkered print)

¾" (2 cm) (pink flower print)

¼" (6 mm)

Pattern B

(pink flower print)

(beige flower print)

¾" (2 cm)   Pattern A

(white flower print)   (green flower print)

(red print)

¾" (2 cm)

¾" (2 cm)

Rocking stitch around each piece

34⅝" (88 cm)

¼" (6 mm)

34⅝" (88 cm)

¼" (6 mm)   ¼" (6 mm)

One layer each: Front Fabric (Patchwork), Batting, Back Fabric (Print)

Cut pieces leaving a ¼" (6 mm) seam allowance.

Prepare 43⁵⁄₁₆" × 43⁵⁄₁₆" (110 × 110 cm) of the back fabric and batting.

Broken Star

Quilt on page 18
Finished Dimensions 36¼" × 36¼" (91.9 × 91.9 cm)
Full-size patterns and appliqué designs: side D (see insert)

Materials

COTTON FABRIC

Seven different prints (Pattern A) (flower, checkered, etc.)	as needed
Two flower prints, striped (Pattern B)	as needed
White flower print (Pieces a, b)	43⁵⁄₁₆" × 19¹¹⁄₁₆" (110 × 50 cm)
Solid white (Piece a)	43⁵⁄₁₆" × 11¾" (110 × 30 cm)
Three prints, green and pink (appliqué fabric)	as needed
Checkered print (binding)	43⁵⁄₁₆" × 7⅞" (110 × 20 cm)
Print (back fabric)	43⁵⁄₁₆" × 43⁵⁄₁₆" (110 × 110 cm)

BATTING

Batting	43⁵⁄₁₆" × 43⁵⁄₁₆" (110 × 110 cm)

Cutting measurements for borders and binding are on the Quilt Diagrams.

Instructions

1. Draw the appliqué designs onto the plain white Piece a, and then sew the appliqué.

2. Sew together the pieces to form the quilt top piece.

3. Draw the quilting lines. Layer the back fabric, batting, and quilt top piece. Baste.

4. Quilt. Trim extra back fabric and batting to the edges of the top piece.

5. Cut the binding fabric to 1⅜" (3.5 cm) wide and 4.2 yd (380 cm) long. Wrap it around the perimeter of the quilt to create a ¼" (6 mm) -wide border and finish.

Quilt Diagram

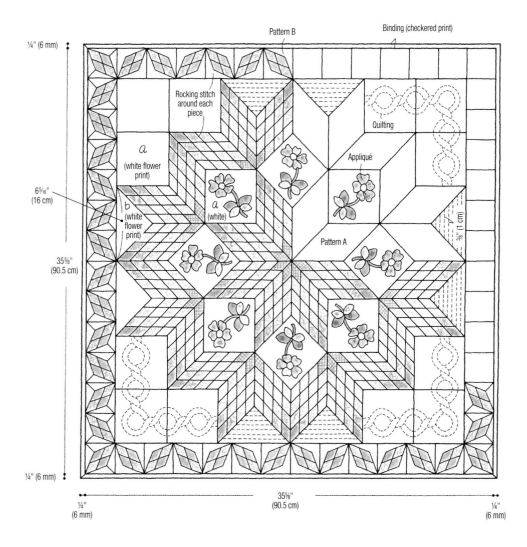

One layer each: Front Fabric (Patchwork), Batting, Back Fabric (Print)

Cut pieces leaving a ¼" (6 mm) seam allowance. Cut appliqué leaving a ⅛" (3 mm) seam allowance.

Prepare 43⁵⁄₁₆" × 43⁵⁄₁₆" (110 × 110 cm) of the batting and back fabric.

Round-Robin Quilts

Flying Swallows

Quilt on page 22
Finished Dimensions 36½" × 36½" (91.4 × 91.4 cm)
Pattern and appliqué designs: side D (see inserts)

Materials

COTTON FABRIC

Assorted prints (pieces, binding fabric)	as needed
Purple hand dyed (pieces, border)	43⁵⁄₁₆" × 60" (110 × 150 cm)
Light purple small flower print (appliqué fabric)	11¾" × 11¾" (30 × 30 cm)
Print (back fabric)	43⁵⁄₁₆" × 43⁵⁄₁₆" (110 × 110 cm)

BATTING

Batting	43⁵⁄₁₆" × 43⁵⁄₁₆" (110 × 110 cm)

HEAVYWEIGHT YARN

White (for trapunto)	as needed

Cutting measurements for borders and binding are on the Quilt Diagrams.

Instructions

1. Position and draw the border appliqué, and then sew the appliqué. Sew the border together into one piece.

2. Make each pattern, then sew them together to form the quilt top piece.

3. Draw the quilting lines on the quilt top piece. Layer the back fabric, batting, and quilt top piece. Baste.

4. Quilt, then trim extra back fabric and batting to the edges of the top piece.

5. Cut the binding fabric to 1⅜" (3.5 cm) wide and 4.2 yd (380 cm) long. Wrap it around the perimeter of the quilt to create a ¼" (6 mm) -wide border and finish.

6. Wash the quilt (see page 75). When it is dry, add the trapunto (see pages 104–105).

Quilt Diagram

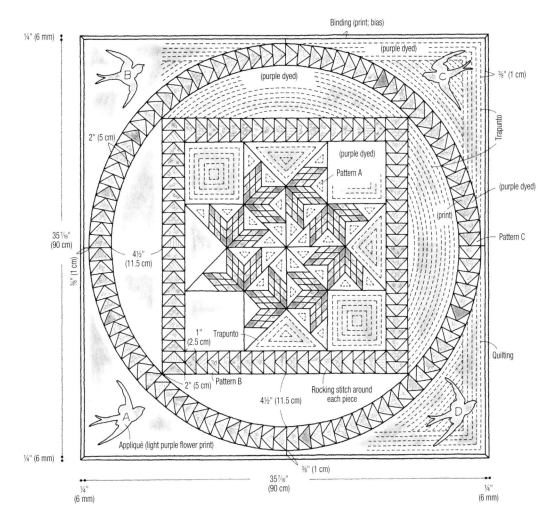

One layer each: Front Fabric (Patchwork), Batting, Back Fabric (Print)

Cut pieces leaving a ¼" (6 mm) seam allowance. Cut appliqué leaving a ⅛" (3 mm) seam allowance.

Prepare 43⁵⁄₁₆" × 43⁵⁄₁₆" (110 × 110 cm) of the back fabric and batting.

Pattern B

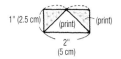

Round-Robin Quilts

Pinwheel Star

Quilt on page 17
Finished Dimensions 36½" × 36½" (91.4 × 91.4 cm)
Pattern and appliqué designs: side C (see insert)

Materials

COTTON FABRIC

White lace (Pattern A)	43⁵⁄₁₆" × 9⅞" (110 × 25 cm)
Five to six prints (Pattern A, B) (purple dot, flower, etc.)	as needed
Light purple flower print (Pattern C, lattice)	43⁵⁄₁₆" × 27½" (110 × 70 cm)
Dark purple dot print (Pattern C)	43⁵⁄₁₆" × 7⅞" (110 × 20 cm)
Solid light blue (border)	23⅝" × 36" (60 × 90 cm)
Pink, green flower prints (appliqué fabric)	as needed
Checkered print (binding)	43⁵⁄₁₆" × 27½" (110 × 70 cm)
Print (back fabric)	43⁵⁄₁₆" × 43⁵⁄₁₆" (110 × 110 cm)

BATTING

Batting	43⁵⁄₁₆" × 43⁵⁄₁₆" (110 × 110 cm)

Cutting measurements for borders and binding are on the Quilt Diagrams.

Instructions

1. Make Patterns A and B, then sew them together to form the center block.

2. Sew the border into one piece. Draw the appliqué design along the border, then sew the appliqué.

3. Sew the lattice and the border from step 2 to the block from step 1. Then sew on Pattern C to complete the quilt top piece.

4. Draw the quilting lines. Layer the back fabric, batting, and quilt top piece. Baste.

5. Quilt, then trim extra back fabric and batting to the edges of the top piece.

6. Cut the binding fabric to 1⅜" (3.5 cm) wide and 4.2 yd (380 cm) long. Wrap it around the perimeter of the quilt to create a ¼" (6 mm) -wide border and finish.

Quilt Diagram

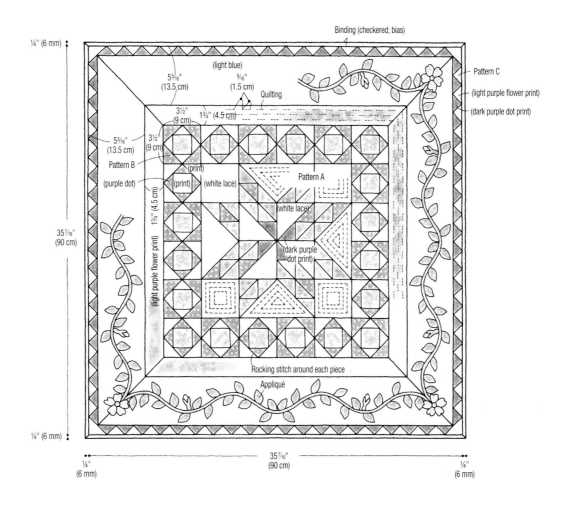

Binding (checkered; bias)

¼" (6 mm)

(light blue)

5⁵⁄₁₆" (13.5 cm)

⁹⁄₁₆" (1.5 cm)

Quilting

3½" (9 cm)

1¾" (4.5 cm)

Pattern C

(light purple flower print)

(dark purple dot print)

5⁵⁄₁₆" (13.5 cm)

3½" (9 cm)

Pattern B

(purple dot)

(print)

(print)

(white lace)

Pattern A

(white lace)

1¾" (4.5 cm)

(light purple flower print)

(dark purple dot print)

35⁷⁄₁₆" (90 cm)

Rocking stitch around each piece

Appliqué

¼" (6 mm)

35⁷⁄₁₆" (90 cm)

¼" (6 mm)

¼" (6 mm)

One layer each: Front Fabric (Patchwork), Batting, Back Fabric (Print)

Cut pieces leaving a ¼" (6 mm) seam allowance. Cut appliqué leaving a ⅛" (3 mm) seam allowance.

Prepare 43⁵⁄₁₆" × 43⁵⁄₁₆" (110 × 110 cm) of the back fabric and batting.

Round-Robin Quilts

Rising Star

Quilt on page 12
Finished Dimensions 36½" × 36½" (91.4 × 91.4 cm)
Full-size pattern and appliqué designs: side D (see insert)

Materials

COTTON FABRIC

Various fabric scraps (pieces)	as needed
Dark red flower print (border, lattice, binding)	43⁵⁄₁₆" × 19¹¹⁄₁₆" (110 × 50 cm)
Solid green and red; pink print (appliqué fabric)	as needed
Print (back fabric)	43⁵⁄₁₆" × 43⁵⁄₁₆" (110 × 110 cm)

BATTING

Batting	43⁵⁄₁₆" × 43⁵⁄₁₆" (110 × 110 cm)

HEAVYWEIGHT YARN

White (for trapunto)	as needed

Cutting measurements for borders and binding are on the Quilt Diagrams.

Instructions

1. Make the square center block, and then sew the appliqué (refer to quilt diagram).

2. Sew the remaining pieces and border together to form the quilt top piece.

3. Draw the quilting lines. Layer the back fabric, batting, and quilt top piece. Baste.

4. Quilt, then trim extra back fabric and batting to the edges of the top piece.

5. Cut the binding fabric to 1⅜" (3.5 cm) wide and 4 yd (370 cm) long. Wrap it around the perimeter of the quilt to create a ¼" (6 mm) -wide border and finish.

6. Wash the quilt (see page 75). When the quilt is dry, add the trapunto to the border and lattice (see pages 104–105).

Quilt Diagram

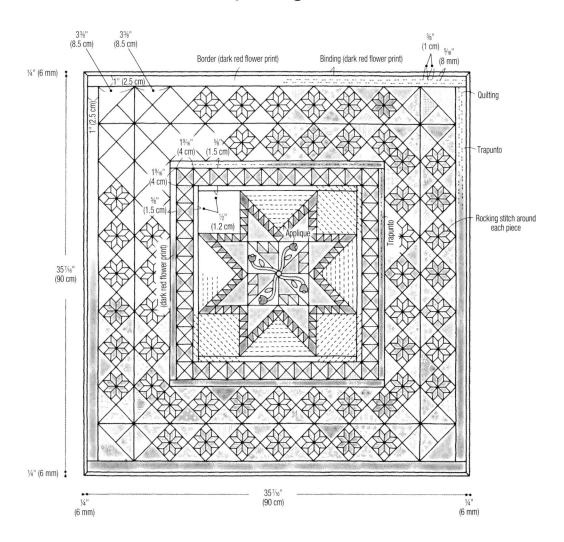

One layer each: Front Fabric (Patchwork), Batting, Back Fabric (Print)

Cut pieces leaving a ¼" (6 mm) seam allowance. Cut appliqué leaving a ⅛" (3 mm) seam allowance.

Prepare 43⁵⁄₁₆" × 43⁵⁄₁₆" (110 × 110 cm) of the back fabric and batting.

Round-Robin Quilts

Eternal Blossom

Quilt on page 16
Finished Dimensions 36½" × 36½" (91.4 × 91.4 cm)
Pattern A: side D (see insert)
Full-size Pattern C: page 81

Materials

COTTON FABRIC

White flower print (Pattern C, D)	43⁵⁄₁₆" × 48" (110 × 120 cm)
Pink print (Pattern B)	43⁵⁄₁₆" × 40" (110 × 100 cm)
Various prints (flower, dot, etc.) (pieces)	as needed
Green print (lattice)	23⅝" × 11¹³⁄₁₆" (60 × 30 cm)
Flower print (lattice, binding)	43⁵⁄₁₆" × 15¾" (110 × 40 cm)
Print (back fabric)	43⁵⁄₁₆" × 43⁵⁄₁₆" (110 × 110 cm)

BATTING

Batting	43⁵⁄₁₆" × 43⁵⁄₁₆" (110 × 110 cm)

Cutting measurements for borders and binding are on the Quilt Diagrams.

Instructions

1. Make each pattern and then sew them together to form the quilt top piece.

2. Layer the back fabric, batting, and quilt top piece. Baste.

3. Quilt using a rocking stitch around each piece. Trim extra back fabric and batting to the edges of the top piece.

4. Cut the binding fabric to 1⅜" (3.5 cm) wide and 4.2 yd (380 cm) long. Wrap it around the perimeter of the quilt to create a ¼" (6 mm) -wide border and finish.

Quilt Diagram

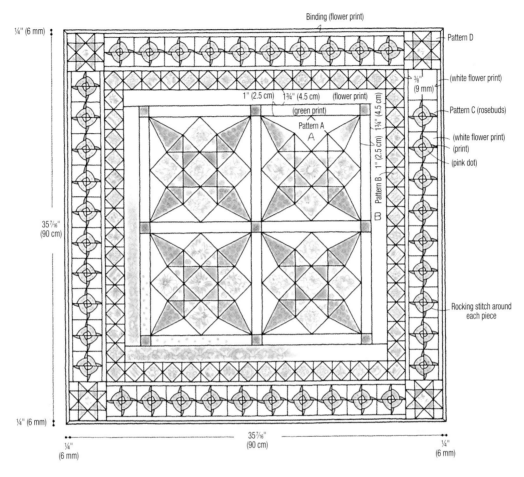

Binding (flower print)

¼" (6 mm)

Pattern D

⅜" (9 mm) (white flower print)

1" (2.5 cm) 1¾" (4.5 cm) (flower print)

(green print)

Pattern C (rosebuds)

Pattern A

A

(white flower print)
(print)
(pink dot)

Pattern B 1" (2.5 cm) 1¾" (4.5 cm)

B

35⁷⁄₁₆" (90 cm)

Rocking stitch around each piece

¼" (6 mm)

35⁷⁄₁₆" (90 cm)

¼" (6 mm) ¼" (6 mm)

One layer each: Front Fabric (Patchwork), Batting, Back Fabric (Print)

Cut pieces leaving a ¼" (6 mm) seam allowance.

Prepare 43⁵⁄₁₆" × 43⁵⁄₁₆" (110 × 110 cm) of the back fabric and batting.

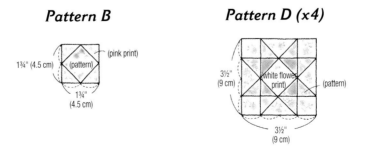

Pattern B

1¾" (4.5 cm) (pink print)

(pattern)

1¾" (4.5 cm)

Pattern D (x4)

3½" (9 cm) (white flower print) (pattern)

3½" (9 cm)

Small Tote

Wandering Diamond

Quilt on page 45

Finished Dimensions 17⅛" × 10" (18.1 × 25.2 cm)

Full-size pattern: side A (see insert)

COTTON FABRIC

Four prints (small flower, striped, light and dark shaded, etc.) (Pieces a, b, c)	as needed
Flower print (light gray embroidered fabric) (Piece d)	11¹³⁄₁₆" × 7⅞" (30 × 20 cm)
Checkered or solid gray (binding)	25⅝' × 3⁵⁄₁₆" (65 × 10 cm)
Red flower print or blue print (zipper pull, handle)	40" × 1" (100 × 2.5 cm)
Print (back fabric)	17¾" × 13¾" (45 × 35 cm)

BATTING

Batting	17¾" × 13¾" (45 × 35 cm)

ZIPPER

Zipper	8¾" (22 cm)

HEAVYWEIGHT YARN

White (for the zipper pull)	as needed

Cutting measurements for borders and binding are on the Quilt Diagrams.

Instructions

1. Sew together pieces to form the quilt top piece (see page 90 for patterns).

2. Draw the quilting lines. Layer the back fabric, batting, and quilt top piece. Baste.

3. Quilt. Trim extra back fabric and batting to the edges of the top piece.

4. Cut the binding fabric to 1⅜" (3.5 cm) wide and 52" (130 cm) long. Wrap it around the perimeter of the quilt to create a ¼" (6 mm) -wide border and finish.

5. Using a backstitch, attach the zipper to the mouth of the piece from step 4. Close the edge of the zipper tape with a featherstitch. (Diagram 1)

6. Fold the entire piece right side out and machine stitch both sides along the side with the binding. Match the edges of the binding and hemstitch together. Insert the loop for the strap on one side and sew together. (Diagram 2)

7. Make the zipper pull, then pass it through the pull tab of the zipper and twist it. Sew the cord to the loop along the edge. (Diagram 3)

Quilt Diagram

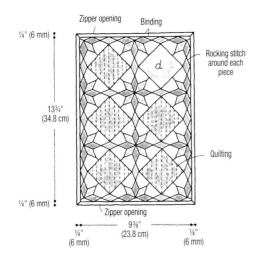

Zipper opening Binding

¼" (6 mm)

13¾"
(34.8 cm)

¼" (6 mm)

Rocking stitch
around each
piece

Quilting

Zipper opening

¼"
(6 mm)

9⅜"
(23.8 cm)

¼"
(6 mm)

Pattern

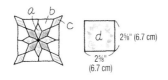

a b

c

d

2⅝" (6.7 cm)

2⅝"
(6.7 cm)

Zipper pull (cotton fabric) x1

1" (2.5 cm)

37⅜"
(95 cm)

Diagram 1

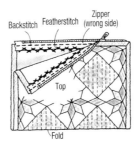

Backstitch Featherstitch Zipper
(wrong side)

Top

Fold

Diagram 2

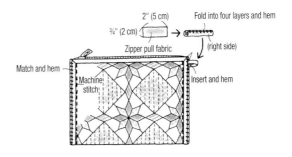

2" (5 cm)

¾" (2 cm)

Fold into four layers and hem

Zipper pull fabric

(right side)

Match and hem

Machine
stitch

Insert and hem

Diagram 3

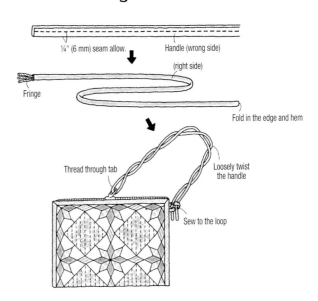

¼" (6 mm) seam allow.

Handle (wrong side)

(right side)

Fringe

Fold in the edge and hem

Thread through tab

Loosely twist
the handle

Sew to the loop

One layer each (Main Body): Front Fabric (Patchwork), Batting, Back Fabric (Print)

Cut pieces leaving a ¼" (6 mm) seam allowance. Cut the handle.

Prepare 17¾" × 13¾" (45 × 35 cm) of the back fabric and batting for the main body.

Quilts on page 40

Finished Dimensions

A 9⅞" × 13¾" (25 × 35 cm)

B 9⅞" × 14⅜" (25 × 36.4 cm)

Full-size pattern for A: side A (see insert)

Full-size pattern for B: page 85

Tote Bags

Shooting Star II (A)

COTTON FABRIC

Six different prints (pieces)	as needed
Checkered print (handle)	13¾" × 7⅞" (35 × 20 cm)
Print (back fabric, finishing for bag opening, and handle)	29½" × 19¹¹⁄₁₆" (75 × 50 cm)

BATTING

Batting	31½" × 17¾" (80 × 45 cm)

Cutting measurements for borders and binding are on the Quilt Diagrams.

Lone Star (B)

COTTON FABRIC

Four different prints, solid pink	43⁵⁄₁₆" × 7⅞" (110 × 20 cm) each
Checkered print (pieces, handle, binding fabric)	19¹¹⁄₁₆" × 27½" (50 × 70 cm)
Print (back fabric, finishing for bag opening, and handle)	29½" × 19¹¹⁄₁₆" (75 × 50 cm)

BATTING

Batting	31½" × 17¾" (80 × 45 cm)

Cutting measurements for borders and binding are on the Quilt Diagrams.

Instructions

1. Sew the pieces to form the quilt top. (For each pattern, see: page 92 for A, page 85 for B, page 94 for C, page 88 for D, and page 86 for E).

2. Draw the quilting lines. Layer the back fabric, batting, and quilt top piece. Baste.

3. Quilt. Trim extra back fabric and batting to the edges of the top piece. (Diagram 1)

4. Fold the quilt inside out and stitch up both sides. Wrap the seam allowance into the back fabric and hem. (Diagram 2)

5. Finish the opening. Cut the binding fabric to 1⅜" (3.5 cm) wide and 31½" (80 cm) long for Totes C and E. Neaten the fabric around the opening (see page 74).

6. Prepare a 31½" (80 cm) -long and 1" (2.5 cm) -wide back fabric for Totes A, B, and D. Align it with the inside of the bag opening and sew. Turn the bag back right side out and hem. (Diagram 3)

7. Make two handles and attach them with a hemstitch at the points. (Diagram 4)

See additional tote bags on page 190.

Quilt Diagrams

Cut pieces leaving a ¼" (6 mm) seam allowance. Cut out handles.

Prepare 31½" × 17¾" (80 × 45 cm) for the back fabric and batting of the main body.

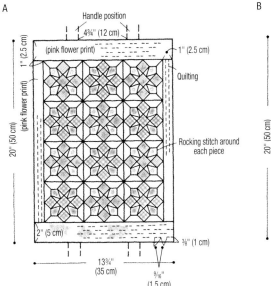

A

Handle position
4¾" (12 cm)

(pink flower print)

1" (2.5 cm)

1" (2.5 cm)

(pink flower print)

20" (50 cm)

Quilting

Rocking stitch around each piece

2" (5 cm)

⅜" (1 cm)

13¾" (35 cm)

9/16" (1.5 cm)

One layer each (A Main Body):
Front Fabric (Patchwork),
Batting, Back Fabric (Print)

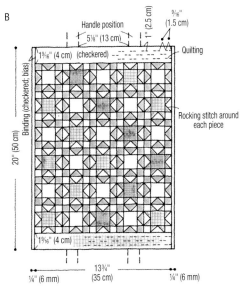

B

Handle position
5⅛" (13 cm)

1" (2.5 cm)

9/16" (1.5 cm)

1 9/16" (4 cm)   (checkered)

Quilting

Binding (checkered; bias)

20" (50 cm)

Rocking stitch around each piece

1 9/16" (4 cm)

¼" (6 mm)

13¾" (35 cm)

¼" (6 mm)

One layer each (B Main Body):
Front Fabric (Patchwork),
Batting, Back Fabric (Print)

Diagram 1

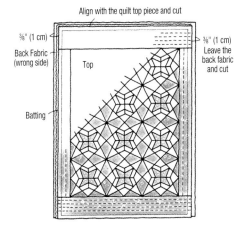

Align with the quilt top piece and cut

⅜" (1 cm)

⅜" (1 cm)

Back Fabric (wrong side)

Leave the back fabric and cut

Top

Batting

Diagram 2

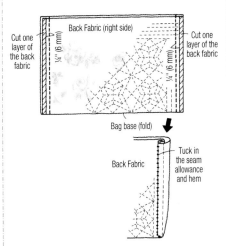

Back Fabric (right side)

Cut one layer of the back fabric

¼" (6 mm)

Cut one layer of the back fabric

¼" (6 mm)

Bag base (fold)

Back Fabric

Tuck in the seam allowance and hem

Diagram 4

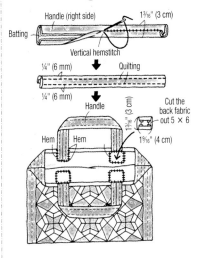

Handle (right side)

1 3/16" (3 cm)

Batting

Vertical hemstitch

¼" (6 mm)

Quilting

¼" (6 mm)

Handle

1 3/16" (3 cm)

Hem

Hem

Cut the back fabric out 5 × 6

1 9/16" (4 cm)

Two of each for the Handle: Front Fabric (Cotton Fabric), Batting

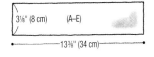

3⅛" (8 cm)   (A–E)

13⅜" (34 cm)

Diagram 3

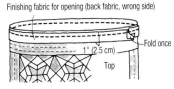

Finishing fabric for opening (back fabric, wrong side)

Fold once

1" (2.5 cm)

Top

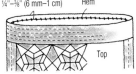

¼"–⅜" (6 mm–1 cm)

Hem

Top

Quilts on page 41

Finished Dimensions

C 11" × 14½" (27.7 × 37 cm)

D 9¾" × 13⅝" (24.8 × 34.7 cm)

E 10" × 13¾" (25.7 × 35 cm)

Full-size patterns for C, D, and E: side A (see insert)

Tote Bags

Milky Way and Log Cabin (C)

COTTON FABRIC

Five different prints (pieces)	as needed
Dark print (pieces, handle, binding fabric)	31½" × 11¾" (80 × 30 cm)
Print (back fabric, finishing for the handle)	23⅝" × 19¹¹⁄₁₆" (60 × 50 cm)

BATTING

Batting	31½" × 17¾" (80 × 45 cm)

Cutting measurements for borders and binding are on the Quilt Diagrams.

Stardust Memory (D)

COTTON FABRIC

Four different prints (pieces)	as needed
Dark print (pieces, handle fabric)	27½" × 59" (70 × 150 cm)
Print (back fabric, finishing for the opening and handle)	29½" × 19¹¹⁄₁₆" (75 × 50 cm)

BATTING

Batting	31½" × 17¾" (80 × 45 cm)

Cutting measurements for borders and binding are on the Quilt Diagrams.

Star Blossom (E)

COTTON FABRIC

Three different prints (pieces, binding fabric)	as needed
Checkered print (pieces, handle fabric)	15¾" × 9⅞" (40 × 25 cm)
Print (back fabric, finishing for handle)	23⅝" × 19¹¹⁄₁₆" (60 × 50 cm)

BATTING

Batting	31½" × 17¾" (80 × 45 cm)

Cutting measurements for borders and binding are on the Quilt Diagrams.

See instructions on page 188

Quilt Diagrams

Cut pieces leaving a ¼" (6 mm) seam allowance. Cut out handles.

Prepare 31½" × 17¾" (80 × 45 cm) for the back fabric and batting of the main body.

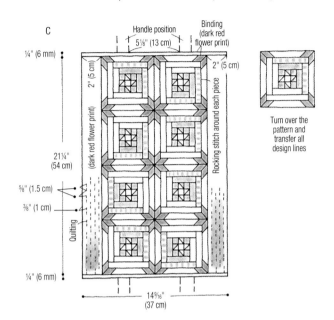

C

Handle position 5⅛" (13 cm)

Binding (dark red flower print)

¼" (6 mm)

2" (5 cm)

(dark red flower print)

Rocking stitch around each piece

21¼" (54 cm)

⅝" (1.5 cm)

⅜" (1 cm)

Quilting

¼" (6 mm)

14⁹⁄₁₆" (37 cm)

Turn over the pattern and transfer all design lines

One layer each (C Main Body):
Front Fabric (Patchwork),
Batting, Back Fabric (Print)

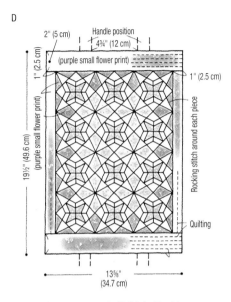

D

2" (5 cm)

Handle position 4¾" (12 cm)

(purple small flower print)

1" (2.5 cm)

1" (2.5 cm)

(purple small flower print)

19½" (49.6 cm)

Rocking stitch around each piece

Quilting

13⅝" (34.7 cm)

One layer each (D Main Body):
Front Fabric (Patchwork),
Batting, Back Fabric (Print)

3⅛" (8 cm) (A–E)

13⅜" (34 cm)

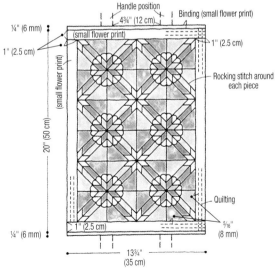

E

Handle position 4¾" (12 cm)

Binding (small flower print)

¼" (6 mm)

(small flower print)

1" (2.5 cm)

1" (2.5 cm)

(small flower print)

20" (50 cm)

Rocking stitch around each piece

Quilting

1" (2.5 cm)

5⁄₁₆" (8 mm)

¼" (6 mm)

13¾" (35 cm)

One layer each (E Main Body):
Front Fabric (Patchwork),
Batting, Back Fabric (Print)

About the Author

Reiko Washizawa is an expert quilter who designs primarily in traditional American quilting styles. She also teaches several techniques, including appliqué and trapunto. She is known for her romantic and delicate quilt designs. She is the author of many books, including *A Life of Patchwork Quilting* (NHK Publication) and *Reiko Washizawa's Patchwork Quilt Home Quilt* (Vogue Japan).